MW00856339

THE LAW OF LOVE

THE LAW OF LOVE

Modern Language for
Ancient Wisdom

RICHARD LEONARD, SJ

Paulist Press
New York / Mahwah, NJ

The Scripture quotations contained herein are from the New Revised Standard Version: Catholic Edition, Copyright © 1989 and 1993, by the Division of Christian Education of the National Council of the Churches of Christ in the United States of America. Used by permission. All rights reserved.

"Light looked down" by John L. Bell from Cloth for the Cradle, Copyright © 1997, 2000, WGRG c/o Iona Community, Scotland. GIA Publications, Inc., exclusive North American agent. 7404 S. Mason Ave., Chicago, IL 60638 www.giamusic .com 800.442.1358. All rights reserved. Used by permission

Cover image from Shutterstock.com
Cover and book design by Lynn Else

Copyright © 2021 by Richard Leonard

All rights reserved. No part of this publication may be reproduced, stored in a retrieval system, or transmitted in any form or by any means, electronic, mechanical, photocopying, recording, scanning, or otherwise, without either the prior written permission of the Publisher, or authorization through payment of the appropriate per-copy fee to the Copyright Clearance Center, Inc., www .copyright.com. Requests to the Publisher for permission should be addressed to the Permissions Department, Paulist Press, permissions@paulistpress.com.

Library of Congress Control Number: 2020947000

ISBN 978-0-8091-5537-8 (paperback)
ISBN 978-1-58768-933-8 (e-book)

Published by Paulist Press
997 Macarthur Boulevard
Mahwah, New Jersey 07430
www.paulistpress.com

Printed and bound in the
United States of America

In gratitude to my family: Joan; Tracey (RIP); Peter and Michelle;
Amy and Pierce; Connor and Hamish; Tom, Tecia, and Felix;
Emily and Pieter; and to Mary, Emma, and Humphrey;
Virginia (RIP) and Fabian (RIP); Kathy and David; Tim and
Angela; Claudia and Roger; Maryanne and Ernest;
Phillip and Caz; Sally and Jack; Dannielle and Christian;
Alex and Peter; and your families,
for your unconditional love.

CONTENTS

PREFACE

In thinking about the law of love, we must face up to the fact that some people balk at the words *law* and *love* being in the same sentence. I understand their hesitation, given that the purest sense of love never carries with it an obligation to a code but is a freely offered gift and an exchange. As we will soon see, the way Jesus and John and Paul use the concept of the law of love is not as a book of rules to obey but as the wellspring that guides all choices, determinations, decisions, and even sometimes duties in our lives. It is not meant to be burdensome and one way, but a reciprocal gift-giving. Here is a story about when that theory became practice in my own life.

My family is not demonstrative. We don't have those "love you darling" signoffs at the end of every phone call. A firm handshake for the men and a peck on the cheek for the women is as good as it gets. During my final high school retreat, I was challenged to "never leave this world not having told the people that you love that you love them." At seventeen, I had never told my mother, brother, or sister I loved them, and they had never said it to me either. My father died when I was two, so I came back from my school retreat on a mission. My sister was then working with Mother Teresa in Calcutta, and my brother was working interstate.

THE LAW OF LOVE

I sat down and wrote them letters telling them that I loved them. I have never had a reply, from either of them!

That left my mother. I stayed in one Saturday night and, after dinner, I was in my bedroom. I was so nervous at what I was about to do, you would swear I was about to ask my mother to marry me. I approached the lounge room where Mum was watching the 7:00 p.m. news. I blurted out, "Mum, I have something very important to tell you." My mother, not taking her eyes from the screen, casually said, "Oh, yes, what's that?" "No," I responded, "I've never told you this before, and it's very important that I tell you tonight."

My mother slowly turned off the TV and turned toward me. Now I could tell there were two hearts pumping and two tummies churning in that room. Decades later my mother told me that she was saying to herself, "Whatever he says next—keep calm, keep calm, keep calm."

I plucked up all my courage and came straight out with it. "Mum, I just want to tell you that I love you." Mum thought it was the warm-up for the big news yet to come.

"Is that it?"

"Yes. Before I die, I wanted to be able to say that I had told you that I love you."

"You're not terminally ill, are you?"

"No, I hope to die an old man, but before then I wanted to tell you I love you."

Such was her relief she said, "Goodness me, I hope so," and promptly turned on the television.

As I walked back to my bedroom I said aloud, "I don't think it was supposed to go like that." There were no violins playing, no warm embraces or statements like, "At least one of you three ingrates has turned up to tell me that you love me."

What did happen was that my brother and my sister wrote to my mother, "We've had these very weird letters from him."

"O, bully for you," my mother replied, "I've had the whole episode in person. But don't worry, it's a phase he's going through."

I hope it's a phase I will never get over, because I am baptized in the love of God made visible in Christ. Following Jesus's example, then, how do we work out who we love? Ask one question: For whom would you die? In my experience that shortens the "I love you" list considerably, and if your dog or cat is seriously on that list, you need therapy immediately. For while we can enjoy our pets, dying for them establishes that our priorities need reordering.

One of the problems is that we now say we love our car, our house, and ice cream, but things can't love us back. Added to this is how we regularly tell people that we don't love that we love them. These days it's often for sex, or we say "I love you" out of obligation or a bad habit, but we don't actually mean it. And because we know that actions are more telling than words, we don't easily believe others when they tell us they love us. We can feel unlovable and cynical about the whole experience, which does not help when God whispers it in our ear continuously. We may not trust God either.

To assist us in reclaiming that we can trust love as the definitive point of the Christian revelation, here are reflections on some of the great biblical texts on the law of love: the Ten Commandments; the Beatitudes; the Lord's Prayer; love God and love your neighbor as yourself; and 1 Corinthians 13, which says that love is kind and patient. The best outcome from this book would be that by its end we agree only to tell the people that we actually love that we love them, and then live out the love we profess. We would change the world.

ACKNOWLEDGMENTS

Mark-David Janus, CSP, Donna Crilly, Bob Byrns, and the team at Paulist Press for their continuing belief in me and my work, and for enabling me to talk to a very wide audience about faith and culture;

Vu Kim Quyen, SJ, Brian McCoy, SJ, and the Australian Province of the Society of Jesus, for the education and formation I have received and their on-going support to do the "greatest good for the greatest number";

the forbearance of my Jesuit community at Lavender Bay, Sydney, whose support and care, at home and while away, provides a home base for a ministry often lived "with one foot in the air."

CHAPTER 1

LOVE IS HIS WORD

Six days later, Jesus took with him Peter and James and his brother John and led them up a high mountain, by themselves. And he was transfigured before them, and his face shone like the sun, and his clothes became dazzling white. Suddenly there appeared to them Moses and Elijah, talking with him. Then Peter said to Jesus, "Lord, it is good for us to be here; if you wish, I will make three dwellings here, one for you, one for Moses, and one for Elijah." While he was still speaking, suddenly a bright cloud overshadowed them, and from the cloud a voice said, "This is my Son, the Beloved; with him I am well pleased; listen to him!" When the disciples heard this, they fell to the ground and were overcome by fear. But Jesus came and touched them, saying, "Get up and do not be afraid." And when they looked up, they saw no one except Jesus himself alone.

(Matt 17:1–8)

1

THE LAW OF LOVE

I am writing this book during the COVID-19 crisis. While this time has given me a welcomed and unexpected space to read and write, it has also offered me an insight to why these meditations are necessary. Over recent weeks I have read Catholic and other Christian leaders say that God has sent COVID-19 as a punishment for various contemporary sins. The implication here is that retribution is God's way, nature, or law. This confirms for me that some Christians have an extremely limited image of the Holy Trinity: nasty God the Father in heaven, lovely Jesus, and the bird!

While we believe in one God in three persons, they act as one in creating, saving, and inspiring. Furthermore in John's Gospel, Jesus says he does nothing on his own (5:30); "the Father and I are one" (10:30); and "whoever has seen me has seen the Father" (14:9). For a Christian everything in the Old Testament is interpreted through the definitive revelation of God in Jesus Christ. I know our Jewish sisters and brothers don't like us saying this, but Jesus not only came to fulfill the Old Testament but also to correct it.

This theology matters when we come to plagues. For the prescientific peoples of the Bible, everything was given a theological reading. If there was a flood, plague, or pestilence, then God was saying something through it. This theology reveals a prescientific belief in a tyrannical God, where bad behavior is tolerated up to a point, but then the nonsense is stopped, and a plague is sent to remind us who's boss. No one loves a tyrant, we survive them as best we can, and in this paradigm God's love and fidelity seems dependent on what we do, which contradicts the nature of God as revealed in Christ, and in what Paul taught in Romans 8.

However, in the Gospels Jesus never sends a plague, a natural disaster, or turns anyone into a pillar of salt. For Christians, then, if Jesus wasn't into murderous retribution, taking him at his repeated word, then neither is God. He was the incarnate correction to false interpretations about how God works in the world. So, even though COVID-19's origins are yet to be finally and scientifically concluded, it has clearly emerged from poor human decisions regarding the created order, not because God has directly sent it upon us.

God as a tyrant is a fearful, neat solution to the deep pain within our lives: suffering has to come from somewhere, and so some argue that it is sent directly by God.

There is a huge difference between a God who permits evil in our world and a God who perpetrates such acts upon us. We believe the first, but you would be forgiven for not knowing that we do not hold to the second. Because God wanted us to have full freedom, we must have the possibility of choosing evil—non-God—or we would be marionettes. But this indirect and more general responsibility is a world away from God directly causing suffering and destruction. Just because many people positively grow through the challenges of pain and suffering, this does not mean God sends these things as a test. Rather, this growth is a testament to God accompanying us through every moment, inspiring us to be in solidarity with all his children, so that together we make the best decisions as we walk in the shadow of death and the valley of tears.

Second, God does not send plagues to teach us things, though we can learn from them—and we are learning a lot right now about our delicate relationship with the created order and how poor choices in one place can affect all places. We are also learning that the best response in tough times is transparency, good government, honest reporting, collective human ingenuity, responsible citizenship, valuing the common good over individuality, and how extraordinarily resilient some of us are in the face of tragedy.

THE LAW OF LOVE

How can I be so confident that God is not deadly by nature and that death, disease, and destruction are not his law or way? Because the God revealed in Jesus Christ was not a tyrant, but a lover who was prepared to go to any lengths to save us even though we did not deserve it. 1 John 1:5 says that "God is light and in him there is no darkness." If that is true, then plagues cannot be part of God's arsenal of weapons to punish us for our sins in this life.

Spiritual sanity rests in seeing that every moment of every day God does what he did on Good Friday, not allowing evil, death, and destruction to have the last word. Through our humility we see that the power of amazing grace enables us to make the most of even the worst situations, help each other in every way we can, and let light and life have the last word. Easter Sunday is God's response to Good Friday: life out of death.

Exploring God's nature is essential before we approach some of the central teachings of our faith and see how they should all be claimed as expressions of God's unconditional love for all of creation. Before COVID-19, the impetus for this book was seeing the way some critics of Pope Francis attacked not just his teachings, but him personally. The public dissenters, along with the keyboard warriors, have held nothing back in their attacks. What has worried me was not just what they said, but the image of God their positions reveal and their approach to the revelation of God in the person of Jesus Christ and in his teachings.

When John XXIII convoked Vatican II, one of the many principles that he hoped would guide the Council was the saying that he wrote in his 1959 encyclical *Ad Petri Cathedram*: "In essentials, unity; in doubtful matters, liberty; in all things, charity." I wonder what he would make of us now. Except that a saint cannot be unhappy in heaven, John XXIII could surely be rolling in his grave.

The petulant critics snapping at Pope Francis, and many

others besides, seem to have as their motto: "In all matters, unity; in doubtful matters, hostility; in no things, charity." I note that these same cardinals, bishops, theologians, and laypeople now throwing stones at the pope were often the ones who sternly lectured the rest of us, from 1978 to 2013, that the litmus test of one's Catholic orthodoxy was public fidelity to the teaching of the Holy Father. How things have changed—for them. The rest of us continue to remain loyal to the See of Peter.

Some of his detractors even cast doubt on the validity of Pope Francis's election. Apparently, either the Holy Spirit abandoned the cardinal electors on March 12, 2013, or she never entered the conclave in the first place. So much for trusting the Lord's promise that he would never abandon his Church until the end of time. Apparently, that only works out if we get the pope we want.

During previous pontificates, I remember being warned against the grave sin of "scandalizing and confusing the faithful." Pope Francis has an extraordinary gift to inspire faith, hope, and love in believer and unbeliever alike. This is in sharp contrast to the nasty taste left by the ugly language of online character assassins, the pompous demands for yes-or-no answers by dubious cardinals, and the pious claims of theologians that they feel forced to point out the pope's errors "out of charity." Could anyone imagine what would have happened to people whose charity impelled them to behave similarly toward St. John Paul II or Benedict XVI? Honest, open, respectful disagreement are essential as we edge closer to the truth through arguments between friends.

The present, not-so-loyal opposition to the pope argues that "error has no rights," which masks an inclination to a creeping infallibility that forecloses debate on issues about which there is legitimate disagreement. This has serious pastoral fallout at the grassroots. One gets the sense that the doctrinal edifice is very shaky indeed—give any ground on anything, and the whole house of cards will come tumbling down. The bottom line for Christians is that every person has rights, even those who hold what we believe is an erroneous position: the right to dignity; to respect; to charity; and to being listened to and interpreted with generosity. If we fail to honor these rights, the evil one is certainly not far away.

Pope Francis has not changed a single element of essential Catholic teaching but challenges us all to reflect on the complexity of every life, the struggles everyone faces, and everyone's need for God's mercy. He invites the Church to look afresh at its pastoral practice and its teaching on peace, social justice, and the environment in the light of Scripture, theology, and tradition, the "signs of the times," and the best science and psychology. We are being called to reclaim the absolute and central revelation of God's love in and through Christ, captured well in Luke Connaughton's hymn, "Love Is His Word":

> Love is His word, Love is His way,
> Feasting with all, fasting alone,
> Living and dying, rising again
> Love only love is His way.

For Christians, following the law of love does not bind us to slavishly follow a set of precepts but to set us free to be the best people we can be. Love for us is a way of being. Christians do not follow laws as such, we follow Christ. This last point matters.

Sometimes we hear preachers and teachers say that the followers of Judaism, Christianity, and Islam are "People of the Book." While Judaism does have the Torah, we have the Bible, and Islam has the Qur'an, Christians do not follow a book. We follow a person. The Word we follow is not in a text but became flesh and blood. Theologian Dan Madigan argues that Christians are not people of the Bible, but of God-in-the-flesh:

> The divine Word is the energy vibrating within everything that has ever been created (John 1:3). And the language God has chosen in order to speak the Word most fully is the language of our own flesh (John 1:14)— "body language" we might say....The Word who came to his own in order to re-establish the primordial relationship between God and humanity (John 1:12) has in the vulnerability of the Cross become most completely flesh, has entered most fully into the human condition, and therefore has united the human and the divine....To the one who showed that divinity is not something to be exploited for oneself, but who poured himself out and humbled himself even to the point of accepting without defense, without retaliation and without recourse to power the unjust sentence of a shameful death....In the resurrection God is not so much overturning and reversing the death of Jesus as affirming it as the expression the truth about divinity. God in effect declares, "This is how I am; this is who I am...affirming the truth not only about divinity but also about humanity: that union of the human and divine in Jesus is opened to all of us. Self-sacrificing love, though it seems to be death-dealing, is revealed as ultimately the way to true life. In living out the same sacrificial love as Jesus did, we too share in his rising to life.[1]

A story highlights this point. For a couple of years, I was the vocations director, the recruitment officer, for the Australian Jesuits. Early on, I decided that our advertisements needed a makeover, so I asked a friend who owned an advertising agency for some help. Free of charge, he gave me a couple of hours with his creative team, whose job it was to brainstorm ideas and come up with creative images and words to get through to the crowded marketplace. This group consisted of seven people between the ages of twenty and thirty-five, who were late to the session. All wore black, chained-smoked even though there were signs up saying "No Smoking," and generally looked bedraggled. Twenty minutes after the appointed start time, the leader of the group asked me, "So in a sentence or two tell us who the market is and what you're trying to sell." I was taken aback as this was a new world for me, but I replied, "Young men between the ages of eighteen and forty who want to give their lives to Christ as a Jesuit in poverty, chastity, and obedience." There was stunned silence. A few moments later the leader dragged heavily on his cigarette, blew out the smoke, and said, "Well that's the hardest f---ing product I've ever had to sell!"

In fact, I went on to have a very spirited conversation with this unchurched group about what Jesuit life entailed and why someone might live it these days. They seemed fascinated and incredulous in equal measure. After two hours they correctly concluded that my "offering in the marketplace" was beyond a pithy slogan or a dramatic visual, so I needed an attention-grabbing tagline that would draw those interested to our website, where our vocation could be explored in more depth. What was the line?

What are you doing on earth for Christ's sake? www.jesuit .org.au

The day our new ad campaign was launched, it was all over the national newspapers and the website crashed, but, sadly, I don't think anyone joined as a result.

When I told the Jesuit community about the language the bright young things in the advertising agency had used regarding our life, they all roared with laughter until an older Jesuit said seriously and truly, "Of course we aren't selling anything. We're offering a way of being in love with Christ, with our sisters and brothers, and with the world." This is what English theologian Martyn Atkins is saying when he says that Christians are not mean to be salespeople for the gospel, we are to be free samples of it (#martynatkins). Again, as Madigan states, "Evangelization is a way of living, a way of incarnating the Word of life, of being the Body of Christ, of embodying the Reign of God—a way of living so inviting and so hospitable that it attracts all those who are looking for a fully human life."[2]

Rowan Williams has also drawn our attention to a central issue in all religious discussions, maybe especially those regarding law, any law, even one to love: power. Given that all religious collectives claim to participate in and channel divine power, Williams argues that this has been corrupted by two things: a projection of human power onto the divine, and mistaking power for control. Williams points out God does not dance to our tune, because we are imperfectly made in God's image and likeness, not the other way around:

> God is not only eternal freedom but eternal bliss... (and) the last thing God needs is people to keep him happy. God is what he is; is what he does; wills what he is, and loves what he wills. A God so imagined is not damaged by our failure. To believe, therefore, in divine power in that way is one step along the road to believing in a divine power which absolves or releases, that is, which makes our failure not the last word. The more clearly and robustly we believe in divine freedom or power or bliss or whatever, the less anxiety you should have about pleasing God....It should be that

kind of pressure or imperative which comes from recognizing that this divine life is the only possible source
for our own bliss or reconciliation or release or absolu-
tion, our own coming to be at home with ourselves
and our world.[3]

How we imagine God's power determines what we believe and
how we behave. I am arguing that God's greatest power is love,
because this was the fundamental power revealed and unleashed
in Jesus Christ.

Love as the defining feature of Christianity was revealed in
one of the first and most dramatic events in Jesus's public ministry: the transfiguration on Mount Tabor. Here is a story to illustrate
its importance to us now.

An American Jesuit theologian, John Powell, in his book
The Challenge of Faith,[4] tells the story of a young man named
Tommy who was resident atheist in his Philosophy of God
class at Loyola University in Chicago. At the end of the course, as
he turned in his final paper, Tommy said to Fr. Powell, "Do you
think I will ever find God?" "No," Powell replied, "but I think God
will find you." Tommy walked away.

Years later, Tommy returned to see John Powell to tell him
that he had been diagnosed with terminal cancer. More than
ever, Tommy said, he wanted to find God, or at least to be in
the right place at the right time to be found by him. John Powell
told Tommy to go and tell the people that he most loved that he
loved them.

Within a week Tommy reported to Fr. Powell that in the midst
of doing this he had a genuine and significant encounter with God.
They had found each other. Tommy died three months later.
John Powell reports that the only way to describe the final three
months of Tommy's life was to say that in the process of telling

others he loved them, he was *transfigured* by God—by divine and human love.

The transfiguration of Jesus is no mountaintop light show. Borrowing heavily from similar stories in the Old Testament, it describes dramatically how loved Jesus was by God and how this experience was seen and known by his disciples.

Most of us will have noticed that in recent years the Church has put much more emphasis on the humanity of Jesus. We can see why. For a long time, Christ's divine nature was often over-emphasized, sometimes at the risk of us thinking of Jesus as God parading around in human form. With new biblical tools more recent scholars started recovering the equally important human nature within Christ. But there can be a danger here as well. Christ can be seen as a man, albeit a good, noble, and selfless man, but simply one of us.

The transfiguration holds both realities together. Mark, Matthew, and Luke, who all recount this event, tell us that Jesus was changed before the eyes of the three disciples. On Tabor, Jesus's divine nature was seen directly and immediately by them, which is why this feast was once called the Manifestation of Divine Glory.

Trying to describe the indescribable, the evangelists use Old Testament shorthand to set the scene: the mountaintop religious experience, a cloud covering them, and the glory of God revealed through dazzling light. Matthew is especially interested in the details of this event because it parallels one of the most important refrains of his Gospel: that Jesus is the new Moses, the fulfillment of the law, and the light that illuminates the darkest night.

As interesting as the similarities are between Moses on Sinai and Jesus on Tabor, the differences are even more revealing. Moses goes up the mountain alone, Jesus takes companions with him who share the experience and witness to it. The face of God is hidden from Moses, whereas on Tabor, Jesus is given to us as the face of God for the world. On Sinai, Moses receives a code of law and is told to make sure the people obey it. On Tabor, Jesus receives a proclamation of God's love, and we're told to listen to him. While Moses's face shines, Jesus's whole body is transfigured with light. Moses descends to enforce the law; Jesus comes down to die that we might live. In fact, Peter, James, and John want to stay on Tabor, but they must come down and start another journey with Jesus to another mountain, to Calvary. They discover the divinity of Jesus in and through his humanity, the uncompromised and uncompromising love of the world's only complete human being.

As for seeing this event as all about externals, I remember teaching a Catholic grade school class on the transfiguration. When I told them what we would be doing, they all beamed, which given the subject matter was an entirely appropriate response. It soon became clear, however, that the kids and I were not on the same page. As soon as I started to talk about Jesus and Mount Tabor, one girl said, "But what about Harry Potter?" What about Harry Potter indeed! When I last read the Gospels, Harry wasn't mentioned. I was then told that in J. K. Rowling's books, when Harry, Ron, and Hermione go to Hogwarts School, they take a course entitled Transfiguration.

In *Harry Potter and the Goblet of Fire*, the class on transfiguration is about spells and charms, mostly for show, where the young magicians perfect their abilities to transform the world around them. They are instructed to be careful about what spells they cast and upon whom, and to make sure that if they transport someone somewhere, they know how to get them back as well. J. K. Rowling saw transfiguration as proof of one's wizarding credentials. In this sense it shares something with the Gospel narrative as well. The disciples are indeed convinced of Jesus's credentials on Mount Tabor, not because of the show of power, but because of the power of love.

The transfiguration shows us that if we want to encounter God then we must experience love. This is not an option for the Christian life. As St. John says in his first letter, "Those who say, 'I love God,' and hate their brother or sister, are liars" (1 John 4:20).

Mount Tabor is not a one-off event for Jesus alone. It is meant to set the pattern for all of us to experience the love of God as sons and daughters through Christ. The problem with the concept of love is that we've devalued the currency. But when it comes to the love of God there are three things of which we can be sure:

- If we feel distant from God, we have only to guess who has moved away from whom. Nothing we do stops God from loving us.
- God loves us as we are, not as we would like to be. As the old saying goes, "You don't have to get good to get God, you have to get God to get good."
- Finally, as the song goes, "You're nobody till somebody loves you." Being loved and loving others is no sentimental exercise, but a participation in the heart of our Christian God, discovering ourselves transfigured by the personal love of God. In the process, God may move from being an idea, an abstraction, even an object of curiosity, to the focus of a loving experience that can give our lives meaning, purpose, and hope. We encounter God's body language in Christ.

The God of Mount Tabor is not interested in each of us feeling isolated as we fulfill the letter of a legal code. God wants all of us to have hearts that listen to the gospel of love so that we can gain the power to transform the world through the sacrifices of our daily lives. If we let it, love can be the defining paradigm through which we understand the revelations contained in the Old Testament, the New Testament, the Christian tradition, and most importantly God's love letter to the world: Jesus Christ. Love changes everything.

CHAPTER 2

THE TEN COMMANDMENTS

Then God spoke all these words:

I am the LORD your God, who brought you out of the land of Egypt, out of the house of slavery; you shall have no other gods before me.

You shall not make for yourself an idol, whether in the form of anything that is in heaven above, or that is on the earth beneath, or that is in the water under the earth. You shall not bow down to them or worship them; for I the LORD your God am a jealous God, punishing children for the iniquity of parents, to the third and the fourth generation of those who reject me, but showing steadfast love to the thousandth generation of those who love me and keep my commandments.

You shall not make wrongful use of the name of the LORD your God, for the LORD will not acquit anyone who misuses his name.

THE LAW OF LOVE

Remember the sabbath day, and keep it holy. Six days you shall labor and do all your work. But the seventh day is a sabbath to the LORD your God; you shall not do any work—you, your son or your daughter, your male or female slave, your livestock, or the alien resident in your towns. For in six days the LORD made heaven and earth, the sea, and all that is in them, but rested the seventh day; therefore the LORD blessed the sabbath day and consecrated it.

Honor your father and your mother, so that your days may be long in the land that the LORD your God is giving you.

You shall not murder.

You shall not commit adultery.

You shall not steal.

You shall not bear false witness against your neighbor.

You shall not covet your neighbor's house; you shall not covet your neighbor's wife, or male or female slave, or ox, or donkey, or anything that belongs to your neighbor.

(Exod 20:1–17)

Many years ago, when I was teaching theology in one of our Jesuit high schools, it was clear that the three parent/teacher sessions held throughout the year were some of the most stressful nights for the staff. Sadly, education has largely moved from being a service to being a commodity: you buy it, and the more people pay, the more they want value-for-money, even to the point of wanting a miracle. Some parents think that because they are paying for an expensive education, it doesn't matter that their child is not gifted in this or that area, is lazy or unmotivated—the school should be able to transform the student into an excellent achiever in all areas. Parent/teacher nights see all this on display, where there is no longer such a thing as an average student, only an average teacher, and everyone has a gifted child. Because Jesuit schools tend to be expensive, some of our parents have unrealistic expectations about what we can do with their child. I know this because the Australian Jesuits are the last Jesuit Province in the world to own and run a winery, Sevenhill Cellars, and at the end of parent/teacher nights, the Jesuits provide wine for the staff. Even those who were normally teetotalers would stay and get smashed. Stress levels were high.

On one of these nights, I was interviewed by the parents of boy to whom I was teaching theology. His father was a high-profile judge, a formidable man. At the beginning of our parent/teacher session, before I could say a word, His Honor pronounced, "We're paying a lot of money for this Jesuit education and my sixteen-year-old boy doesn't even know the Ten Commandments."

"That's terrible," I replied, "Why haven't you taught them to him at home over all these years? I assume everything else is up on the fridge door, so why haven't they been there too?" The judge was speechless. I was just warming up.

"I'm all for everyone knowing them off by heart, but I am much more interested in seeing all of us live them out, so that we don't just know them by rote but that they are written on our hearts. It's also good to remember that Jesus summarized the entire Mosaic Law in his three new commandments: 'To love God with all our heart, mind, and soul, and to love our neighbor as we love ourselves.'"

After some awkward silence, His Honor's wife smiled and said to her husband, "Darling—I assume the case for the prosecution now rests."

I am sorry to shock anyone, but in fact, there are not just Ten Commandments. More surprising still, in the Bible they are only called the Ten Commandments three times (Exod 34:28; Deut

THE LAW OF LOVE

4:1; 10:4). They are sometimes called the Decalogue from two Greek words, *deka* meaning "ten" and *logos* meaning "word": ten words. The Decalogue is a summary of the 613 commandments in the Mosaic Law, and a very helpful summary indeed.

There are two versions of the Ten Commandments: Exodus 20:1–17 and Deuteronomy 5:4–21, and the extensive Mosaic law is given out throughout the Books of Exodus, Leviticus, Numbers, and Deuteronomy, covering everything from murder, stealing, dietary laws, skin diseases, menstruation, to temple laws. The only way to truly do justice to the Ten Commandments is to place them in this context, and to read them against the whole of law of Israel. But many Christians want to pick and choose which Old Testament laws they like and which ones they are very happy to discard. It usually ends up supporting their anxieties or bigotry. Let me give you an example.

Israel Folau is an exceptionally gifted and highly paid Tongan/Australian rugby (football) player. He was once a Mormon but is now a devout member of the biblically fundamentalist The Truth of Jesus Christ Church. It has thirty members, and his father is the pastor. A few years ago, Israel created a storm on Instagram during a Q&A: "Izzyfolau what was gods [*sic*] plan for gay people??" Folau replied, "HELL [*sic*]...unless they repent of their sins and turn to God." Later he explained that the law of God was very clear, and he quoted Leviticus 18:22, "You shall not lie with a male as with a woman; it is an abomination." All hell broke loose. I find it hard to get my head around the extraordinary rumpus people who don't even believe in heaven and hell kicked up over Folau's idiosyncratic opinions regarding who is going where in the next life. Personally, I leave the matter of eternal condemnation up to a merciful and loving God.

In profoundly secular Australia, where religion is often publicly portrayed as irrelevant, this rugby player's theological position threatened to derail his career, jeopardize valuable corporate sponsorship for the Rugby Union franchise, and challenge the right of individuals to free speech. While Israel Folau has every right to say what he believes, he also must take responsibility for what he says.

However, this case highlights the problem with taking the law of the Old Testament literally anymore. It comes back to bite you hard. Mr. Folau is heavily tattooed. It seems he hasn't read or doesn't like Leviticus 19, where, in a long list of things that will condemn us, tattoos are singled out for special mention (Lev 19:27–28). Fundamentalists shouldn't get to pick and choose. Unless people are going to state that they only interpret the laws about sexuality strictly, then we actually find a lot of other things are condemned: eating shellfish (Lev 11:10); having a haircut (Lev 19:27); eating or touching pork, bacon, and ham (Lev 11:7–8); having bodily discharges (Lev 15:1–3—though I'm not sure how we would stop them all!); consulting a medium, spiritualist, or astrologer (Lev 19:31); gossiping (Lev 19:16); cross-fertilization of animals and plants (Lev 19:19); and clothes made of more than one fiber.

The so-called Ten Commandments distinguished the Jews from the other religions around them. Emerging over four thousand years ago, Judaism was almost unique in the ancient world in being monotheistic. There was one God, and moreover, Israel's God had chosen a people as his own and sought out personal and collective relationships with them. God loved Israel so much that he entered into a covenant with them, binding himself to them forever. But the relationship was mutual, so from the beginning God revealed the Torah to guide Israel in its day-to-day living, and to be the basis of all Jewish culture and traditions. To be fair to Jewish history, the mid-third-century translation of the Old Testament, the Septuagint, rendered the Hebrew word *Torah*

THE LAW OF LOVE

into the Greek words *nomos* or *nomia*, denoting "unchanging law." Most Jewish and Christian scholars today believe *teaching* to be a fairer translation of the Hebrew *Torah*. However, it remains true that this teaching was never meant to change but has always been interpreted for times and places. Housed within the first five books of the Bible, the Torah was the sacred instruction and guidance on the covenant between God and the chosen people and how it was to be lived.

The God of the covenant rewarded good behavior and punished the bad. While parts of the Old Testament are exquisitely tender, loving, and forgiving, the God of the Torah could be tough, erupting in rage, jealousy, and anger at legal infringements in big and small matters. Every one of the 613 teachings in the Torah seemed to matter equally. They were about life and death, and there was very little hierarchy in their importance and application. This was corrected later in the way it was interpreted by the rabbinic schools.

Often what these instructions enshrined were hard-won lessons from human experience. Some of them are bound to a time and place. I have no trouble believing that at some stage pre-scientific people ate bad shellfish and infected pork and died. Maybe this happened en masse and often. If everything came from God as a reward or a punishment, it's not hard to see how the dietary laws emerged. The same occurs with thinking that menstruating women were unclean because they bled, that gay people did not have the children that were essential for Israel's survival, and that lepers had to be separated from the community.

As we have progressed in understanding physiology, disease control, and sexuality, the laws given by God in the Bible have been challenged by other evidence-based explanations that have set most of us free from the demands of almost all the Torah—except the Ten Commandments. The Decalogue has transcended fashion and favor for thousands of years. I argue that even though the original expression of these laws is in the negative, each of them enshrines a universal and loving positive. The problem is that the language doesn't work anymore because cultural customs have changed dramatically. The idea of "coveting" anything, but especially "wives, slaves, ox, and ass," highlights the need for a makeover.

In an article entitled "Sinai of the Times," writer and journalist Bryan Appleyard tells how he was struck by how many "ten commandments" govern everything in modern life from management theory, to golf etiquette, to sales. The term is invoked everywhere, not for the content of the original Decalogue, but for authority and seriousness. All this led Appleyard to go back to the first Ten Commandments and see if they had anything to offer.

> Nowadays we don't have universal rules…modern morals tend to be entirely subjective and limited only at the outermost margins by the objective reality of the existence of other people. So the only viable commandment becomes: do what you like as long as it doesn't hurt anyone else.…The problem is that individuals are narrow minded and short-sighted. They don't see the big picture. Any entirely individual morality is likely to be wrong headed and ultimately destructive.[1]

Appleyard, though not a religious man, set out to see if the four-thousand-year-old Decalogue could be given a new language in a way that reclaimed its power and insightfulness into the human condition:

- "I am the LORD your God, who brought you out of the land of Egypt, out of the house of slavery; you shall have no other gods before me." Appleyard says this basically means *Be serious.*

- "You shall not make for yourself an idol, whether in the form of anything that is in heaven above, or that is on the earth beneath, or that is in the water under the earth." *Get real.*
- "You shall not make wrongful use of the name of the LORD your God, for the LORD will not acquit anyone who misuses his name." *Be humble.*
- "Remember the sabbath day, and keep it holy." *Be quiet.*
- "Honor your father and your mother, so that your days may be long in the land that the LORD your God is giving you." *Respect age.*
- "You shall not murder." *Do not kill, for all murder is suicide.*
- "You shall not commit adultery." *Mean what you say.*
- "You shall not steal." *Do not steal, or all the world will die.*
- "You shall not bear false witness against your neighbor." *Honor others, their frailties are usually your own.*
- "You shall not covet your neighbor's house; you shall not covet your neighbor's wife, or male or female slave, or ox, or donkey, or anything that belongs to your neighbor." Appleyard concludes that in today's language this means, *Be kind, be generous, and don't sleep around.*[2]

There is nothing old fashioned about these challenges. As in other instances, we can see that it's not what our tradition has to say, but sometimes it is the way we say it that is the problem.

Even those who don't like religion could easily say yes to Appleyard's makeover of the Ten Commandments because what he has done here is recraft ten ancient prohibitions into statements about how to love, or what to avoid if you want to love. I think he captured a way for Christians to reclaim the Decalogue as an expression of love.

BE SERIOUS

To make my point I simply want to tell you a true story about how we end up taking transitory things too seriously, hoping that these passing things can save us or give us lasting joy. Sometimes the ephemeral even crashes into the Christian story.

In the UK in 2014, the Mulberry Bag Company produced an ad showing a wealthy family opening gifts on Christmas morning. A Kiera Knightley look-alike opens her first present: a personally painted portrait of her done by her sister. "Did you do this?" "Yes, it took me ages." Her mother then hands her a large red box, and once she takes off the lid, up jumps the cutest little puppy, who lovingly gazes at his new owner. "He waves," says Mum. The puppy performs on command. The woman's boyfriend goes to the large French doors and knocks on the pane. A stunning white horse approaches the window. The young woman squeals in delight. "Wait!" he says, and as the horse gets closer, we discover it has a long white horn. "It's a unicorn," he says smugly. Everyone rolls their eyes. Nana puts her champagne down and retrieves her large, clumsily wrapped gift from the top of the grand piano and presents it to her granddaughter. The other relatives snigger with amusement.

When she carefully unwraps the package, a large, red Mulberry bag at last comes forth. The young woman immediately jumps up. "Shut—up! Oh my God! Yes! Yes! I love it," and with spasms of joy, dances around the room hugging the bag and showing it to her family: "Look at it! Look at it!" The unicorn walks away. The puppy gets back into his box. We cut to Grandma, who knows she's won this year's competition, and as she raises an eyebrow with a sly smile to the camera, up comes #winchristmas. The Mulberry logo appears, with the tag line "Find the perfect gift." This ad drew public derision.

The following Christmas, either trying to court the controversy or to stem it, Mulberry produced another ad with the same red bag. This time a young couple are in a small, unfurnished, simple room (stable) with a single exposed lightbulb above their heads (the star). Sitting on the floor, the man says, "I know we weren't giving presents, but here." And with great care places a Mulberry box in front of his wife. As an angelic choir strikes up, Mary says, "Oh my God, Joe, oh…," carefully opens the box and removes a large red Mulberry bag. "It's the most beautiful thing I have ever seen in my life. It's absolutely amazing." The bag's buckle reflects light onto Mary's face. They kiss.

Just then a shepherd turns up. "Evenin'. I heard you had a new bag." And on seeing the bag says, "Lordy, Lordy," and takes the bag into his arms. Just then another shepherd arrives with two sheep, and as he kneels next to his friend, the bag is gently passed into his arms. "I wouldn't normally go for red, but that really works doesn't it? Someone's a very lucky girl."

Next in are three businessmen who arrive in suits wearing the paper party crowns we get in Christmas crackers. "Sorry, the traffic was a nightmare, but we come bearing gifts." And with that they hand over a bottle of wine, food, and perfume. The bag is reverently passed to them and each man holds it with awe. "This is truly marvelous." "It smells amazing." "A thing of wonder. Stupendous!" As the choir crescendos, Joe says, "Guys—it's just a bag" at which the soundtrack abruptly stops and everyone looks at him in disbelief. The tension is broken as Joe laughs and the choir returns; they all silently gaze upon the bag, which is now center stage on the table. The camera tilts up to the exposed light bulb, glowing like a star. The graphic reads, "It's Christmas. What are you worshipping? Christmas starts with Christ."

We can't keep worshipping multiple gods. The Trinity who loved us into life should be enough for all of us.

GET REAL

If we believe in God, then it follows that we must get real about the demands that living the law of love will make on us. Most probably the Israelites turned to idol worship because they could see idols. While images and words are essential in capturing human experience, they point to rather than replace religious encounter. Some atheists claim that our religious experience leads one to believe in "imaginary friends" and helps bolster a fragile sense of who we are and why we are here, that faith is a coping mechanism for those of us who need a crutch to get through life.

Many of them claim it is irrational to believe in anything other than what a scientific method can experiment on, test, evaluate, prove, or disprove, and provide empirical proof for or against. There are two responses to these challenges, which define our religious reality. The first is that there are different types of knowledge: the traditional intelligence quotient (IQ), emotional intelligence, social intelligence, and the even more recent and more contested spiritual intelligence, which is about compassion and creativity, self-awareness and self-esteem, and flexibility and gratitude.

THE LAW OF LOVE

The second response is that there are many human experiences that we are unable to "scientifically" test but in which we believe and trust. The best example of course is love, especially sacrificial love, where a believer or nonbeliever will give everything, even his or her life, for something or someone else. Love can be totally irrational: what we love, who we love, how we love, and why we love. Love and its effects can be observed, but testing, evaluating, proving, or disproving love as an experience tests the limits of empirical knowledge. The same applies to forgiveness, beauty, and conscience. We know these primal human experiences to be real, powerful, and determinative, based on their presence or absence in our lives. When we have a religious experience, we go from being in the group to understanding why the group exists in the first place.

BE HUMBLE

The word *humility* must be one of the most misused and abused in the English language. Its direct antecedent is from the Latin word meaning "low" and quickly came to mean to be in a lowly state. However, the root word for *homilies* is from the word *humus*, which means "of the soil" or "to be grounded." I think it is this earliest definition that provides for a fresh understanding. Most of us have been given wrong ideas about humility, that it is about feeling bad about ourselves, putting ourselves down. I had a teacher at school whose ultimate insult to us when she thought any of us were "getting above our station" was to say sarcastically, "Do you drink your own bath water and kiss yourself good night?" It always stung. But this is not true humility, not even in the Bible.

A careful reading of the story of Adam and Eve in Genesis reveals that the original sin of humanity is wanting to be God.

The serpent seduces Adam and Eve by saying that God knows that if they eat the fruit from the tree of knowledge of good and evil, then they will know everything; in other words, the temptation offered by the evil serpent is to be on the same level as God. Their disobedience is not just to go against God's command (who in the logic of the story has to know they will do this anyway, but then seems surprised and angry when they do), but to compromise their own humanity. They were warned not to eat the fruit of that tree because as human beings they cannot bear the weight of the burden that comes with knowing everything. Brilliantly, Genesis names what humanity wants: the very power we cannot cope with possessing—to resist the frailty and fallibility of being a human being, to be my own God in my life and potentially in the world's as well.

The founder of the Jesuits, St. Ignatius Loyola, knew that humility and power were linked and were the antithesis of love. He thought that to be truly humble was to avoid being seduced by power, riches, and greed, and to use whatever gifts we have received to build up the entire human family. Ignatius thought there were three degrees of humility: the first degree is found in those who live a good life so as to attain heaven; the second degree is in those who live a good life in order to bring faith, hope, and love to bear in our world in a way that liberates others as it has liberated them; finally, the third degree is in those who want to be like Christ in every way, serving the poor and being prophets, prepared to take rejection and insults in order to point to a greater love. Ignatius thought each degree had a good outcome, and while we should strive for greater humility, he recognized that it was a God-given gift as well. If we want to love others, he knew we needed to wage war on our sense of entitlement and simply be grateful for everything. We did not create the world; we inherited it and, as a start, that should make us profoundly grateful.

Ignatius went from being a vain, violent, aimless egotist to knowing that the desire to be a faithful, hopeful, and loving follower of Christ was the best way to live. His conversion is enshrined in his *Prayer for Generosity*:

> Take hold of me Lord.
> Accept this offering of freedom, of memory, of mind,
>   of will.
> These I cling and count as my own.
> All are your gifts, Lord, now I am return them.
> They are yours. Do as you will.
> Give me only your free gift of love.
> In this you give all; in this you give all.
>
> (translation by Daniel Madigan, SJ)

Ignatius tells us that if we have true humility and let go of wanting to be God, and allow God to be God in our lives, it does not mean that God then does all the work. It means that God treats us as adults, in a mutual and loving relationship where, with God, we live grounded lives, knowing that we are creatures, not the Creator, and we have to keep it real!

BE QUIET

Have you noticed how many people answer the question "How are you?" by saying, "I'm tired, exhausted, finished, or spent." And that's the day they come back from holidays! Alternatively, they say, "I'm frantic, run off my feet, there are not enough hours in the day." We all seem to be frantic or exhausted. How do we know this? When was the last time you asked a friend how they were, and heard, "I've got the life/work balance perfectly in order—thanks for asking"? We never hear that. I wonder what would happen if we replied, "Relaxed and laid back" or "Taking time to smell the roses." I don't think we would be believed, or we might get a lecture from our friends on how lucky we are not to be busy!

Sometimes we compete over who can be the most exhausted and the most frantic. I have a friend who always has to be the busiest person he knows. If I ever say I have been busy lately, he will reply, "You're busy? *You're* busy? I'm run off my feet!" And I want to say, "John, I'm sorry, I should've realized we're playing the 'I'm the busiest person in the room competition' and I know you always have to win that one."

As Christians we must be careful about this busyness competition. Being active in our lives and engaged with the world around us is a gift, but if we are honest about our busyness, we must admit some of it is not virtuous. It's about denial, avoidance, or trying to keep up with our peer group. It's curious, isn't it, that just as we all compete to be the busiest person we know, we also complain that what we really want is "some peace and quiet." We can't have it both ways. Compulsive frantic activity is the enemy of peace.

Sometimes we might think that peace and quiet means sitting in the lotus position in a darkened room. It can be, but Christ's gift of peace is more robust than that. Peace is like all the best things in life: an attitude of mind and a habit born of consistently making good choices. Some people can do a large amount of work and be quite serene about it. Peace, for them, is a way of life, of being a contemplative in action.

Seneca, a first-century philosopher, noticed that most of his friends and acquaintances lacked peace. He wrote a famous book on anger and how to deal with it. He especially noticed that his richest friends were the angriest of all. Seneca came to believe that the reason so many people were agitated was that they had unreasonable expectations about how smoothly their day would go. Those who were rich thought their money would buy them an easier life in every way, so when it didn't, they were the angriest of all. If Seneca is right and we want more peace and quiet, then we must have realistic expectations of each day and factor in the things that might go wrong.

If keeping the Sabbath holy means we come to the quiet if only just once a week, or much more than that, then we will live more contemplative lives away from the Sabbath. It can change our lives for the better.

RESPECT AGE

My mother doesn't like Mother's Day very much. I grew up hearing her say, "A sincere thank you most days is infinitely better than a fuss one day of the year." Mother's and Father's Days were not, as is sometimes claimed, invented by department stores to increase sales, but to honor mothers and fathers because we never know how long we will have them with us.

In fact, Mother's Day has only been around since Anna Jarvis began to campaign for it after her own mother died in 1905. By 1908 it was a public holiday in her hometown of Grafton, West Virginia. It caught on in other U.S. states, and in 1914 President Woodrow Wilson declared Mother's Day a national holiday; from there it spread around the world. Maybe unsurprisingly, Father's Day also began in 1908 on July 5 in Fairmont, West Virginia. It was organized by Mrs. Grace Golden Clayton. She was inspired to honor the 210 fathers who had died in a mining tragedy at

Monongah, West Virginia, on December 6, 1907. Grief for lost parents motivated the founders of both days.

The commandment to respect age is not about the calendar but about valuing wisdom and experience. In recent years, biblical scholars have rediscovered the importance of how the Spirit in Old Testament is often called Wisdom, a feminine verb. Wisdom is the personification of God's action in the world.

> For wisdom is more mobile than any motion;
> because of her purity she pervades and penetrates all
>   things....
> Although she is but one, she can do all things,
> and while remaining in herself, she renews all things;
> in every generation she passes into holy souls
> and makes them friends of God, and prophets....
> She is more beautiful than the sun....
> Compared with the light she is found to be superior,
> for it is succeeded by the night,
> but against wisdom evil does not prevail.
> She reaches mightily from one end of the earth to the
>   other,
> and she orders all things well.
>
> (Wis 7:24, 27, 29–30; 8:1)

To encounter Wisdom was to encounter God. Later the word *Wisdom* was translated into Greek as *Sophia*. John's Gospel speaks of the Logos, or Word of God, becoming flesh in Jesus, but an equally strong argument can be made that it was Sophia, or God's Wisdom, that became incarnate.

Older people are not automatically wise, because wisdom comes from reflecting on experience and learning from it. However, contemporary society so overvalues the youth culture that older people and their true wisdom are often overlooked. Respecting age is an interplay between memory and gratitude. Memory is an integral part of being human. I have done several funerals of people who had suffered from Alzheimer's disease. These are rarely very sad occasions because the family invariably says that they "lost" their loved one months or years ago. Why? Because increasingly their loved one couldn't remember anyone or anything. We hold to caring for the body from the womb to the tomb because we believe that human dignity must always be respected.

I am not arguing that people who have lost their memories are less human, because every human being has inalienable rights. Indeed, even if memory seems to have passed externally, maybe it is functioning on a deeper, unconscious level. There are now theories about how even the memories of our conception and birth have a bearing on the way we live our lives. It is also apparent that even when people seem to have lost their memory or are unconscious, they recognize some things at a very deep level. Valuing people's memories is important theologically. When I meet God face-to-face, I will remember who I am and how I lived, and that God will remember me. It's also a comfort for us to think that we will be reunited with those we have loved who died before us, because we remember each other.

The second element in respecting age is gratitude. I think *please* and *thank you* could be the two fastest disappearing words from the English language. In almost every country in the world, the debt we owe to previous generations is vast: the hard work, courage, and sacrifices of our older people have paved the way for what we often take for granted. On nearly every world lifestyle indicator, even if the going is tough at present, we live in the most privileged of circumstances. As Christians, we do not think this is our right, our due, or our good fortune. As Christians, we know this is a blessing, won by the hard work of previous generations, and we respond to it by just being grateful. I could not imagine showing greater respect for anyone than being grateful, to value their hard work and reflective memory.

DO NOT KILL, FOR ALL MURDER IS SUICIDE

It is hard to imagine an issue that divides our communities so sharply as the call to care for our environment. We can already see how the destruction of creation has led to dramatic changes to climate, species, air and soil quality, and rising oceans. For believers, care of the earth can never be seen as new, trendy, or "left wing." The Bible is filled with images, calls, and challenges to live in harmony with the created order. Rain, snow, seeds, sowers, fertile soil, and a laboring creation giving birth to the fruits of the Spirit are just some of the rich grounds upon which we reflect on the importance of our earth's ecology.

Pope Francis has said the care of our common home is *the* right-to-life issue. By saying this he is not diminishing other right-to-life issues but making the unexceptionable point that if we don't have a healthy planet, then none of us will be alive at all. In his letter on the environment, *Laudato Si'*, he gave voice to our obligations not to murder creation, and that we have grave moral obligations to care for creation and to treat it as the gift it is:

- "If the simple fact of being human moves people to care for the environment of which they are a part, Christians in their turn realize that their responsibility within creation, and their duty towards nature and the Creator, are an essential part of their faith." (no. 64)

THE LAW OF LOVE

- "Our insistence that each human being is an image of God should not make us overlook the fact that each creature has its own purpose. None is superfluous. The entire material universe speaks of God's love, his boundless affection for us. Soil, water, mountains: everything is, as it were, a caress of God." (no. 84)
- "A healthy relationship with creation is one dimension of overall personal conversion, which entails the recognition of our errors, sins, faults and failures, and leads to heartfelt repentance and desire to change." (no. 218)
- "The universe unfolds in God, who fills it completely. Hence, there is a mystical meaning to be found in a leaf, in a mountain trail, in a dewdrop, in a poor person's face. The ideal is not only to pass from the exterior to the interior to discover the action of God in the soul, but also to discover God in all things." (no. 233).

Rather than thinking of his teaching as exotic, we can see that our care for the earth is one way we can all refrain from killing creation and by extension murdering peoples and places unknown and unseen, so that the earth is developed in such a way that there will be a productive earth for future generations to inherit. This care for the environment is an important part of our Christian commitment to justice, part of the seamless garment in our ethic of life. If this means we must limit our consumption, change our priorities regarding energy and trade, and show the Third World the way in developing eco-friendly industries, then all the better for us.

Most of us know that we cannot keep going as we are, making ever-increasing unsustainable demands on our planet. There is no point in any of us crying over the future demise of our environment if we do nothing to help it now. Every small thing we do—from being conscious of the issues, to recycling and using our cars less—is important. Some of us are in positions to do a lot more than this, and we should take our Christian responsibilities here very seriously. We cannot be irresponsible about the world's finite resources, hoping that we will find solutions in the future. Avarice is not one of the seven deadly sins for nothing. If for no other reason than self-interest for the future of our family and friends, we must be stewards, not wreckers, of God's good gifts.

MEAN WHAT YOU SAY

Most people we know and love are never forced to take vows, but all the vows we take are within a context. As far as I am aware, we can assume that throughout the world there is nothing in civil law regarding marriage that mentions the word *love* in describing this social institution. It would be hard for the state to legally mandate an emotion, because if it did and if that emotion was absent, then the marriage would be invalid. The state also must make provision for arranged marriages, where the best hope is that love will develop later. Second, while much civil marriage legislation speaks of marriage as a "lifelong commitment," the state makes ample provision for quick and no-fault divorce. The lifelong character of civil marriage is at best a hope. While marriage law often speaks of the couple "forsaking all others," adultery has been decriminalized in every Organization for Economic Co-operation and Development member country except the United States, where it remains a criminal offense in twenty-one states, but prosecutions are so rare that the force of these laws is nil. Finally, as unromantic as it may be, civil marriage law is contract law. As long as each party is of age, under no coercion, of full reason, and knowledgeable what the civil commitment demands, then they can sign the marriage contract. The couple is not actually married in the eyes of the state when the celebrant says so, but when they sign the forms. For that document to be legal, all that is required is that some of the vows are made before an authorized notary or celebrant, usually with two witnesses of legal age.

In many industrialized countries well over 70 percent of all marriages are celebrated in a civil setting, rather than a church, temple, or synagogue. Nonetheless, the state asks the couple to say something like this: "I ask the people, here present, to witness that I, John Smith, take you, Ann Black, to be my lawful wedded wife." That's it! The Church often adds something like "I promise to be true to you, in good times and in bad, in sickness and in health, for better or worse, for richer or poorer. I will love you and honor you all the days of my life." The problem now is that with the proliferation of divorce, often sought for very good reasons, meaning what we say is temporary and contingent, only meant until I mean something else. Commitments are subjective and passing. However, not meaning what I say can destroy love and lives.

During World War II, my Aunt Mercia was one of hundreds of Australian women who fell in love with an American soldier. She married her Episcopalian (Anglican) army captain at the side altar of the St. Stephen's Cathedral, Brisbane, in 1945. He was dashing and handsome, and by the time he had to return to the United States in 1946, they were expecting their first child.

Upon arrival at her new home, Mercia found that her brave solider was not as fearless as she thought. He was completely dominated by his aristocratic Episcopalian mother, who made it clear from the beginning that she opposed their marriage. Mercia's life in that family was a nightmare. The tensions boiled over when Andrew was born. Regardless of the promises the soldier had made in Australia to have their children baptized Catholics, he did not stand up against his mother, who declared that if any grandchild of hers was baptized a "papist" she would disinherit the three of them. The Captain surrendered to his mother and demanded that Andrew be baptized an Episcopalian.

Mercia was devastated. She gathered her few possessions, had her newborn son hastily baptized a Catholic, and fled back to Australia. In 1950, by now a divorcée, she met Ken, a wonderful man who wanted to marry her and be a father to Andrew. When they went to see the local monsignor, he told them they could not be married in the Church, and if they contracted a civil marriage, they would be excommunicated. Things were tough in those days—her Catholicism was one of the reasons Mercia left the United States. In turn, the very Church she had defended now shut her out. From 1951 until 1993, Aunty Mercia and her second husband did not receive any of the sacraments. After attending Mass each week for the first twenty-three years of their marriage but not receiving holy communion, they stopped practicing their faith. Who could blame them?

After I started studying canon law in 1989, I encouraged Mercia to instigate annulment proceedings. She did so in 1990. In 1993, her marriage to her army captain was declared null because he had not meant what he said. A month later, Mercia and Ken were finally married in the Catholic Church at a nuptial Mass. The small congregation knew that this couple had been excluded from the Church for far too long. But we also knew that God had never moved away from them. At that nuptial Mass, Uncle Ken's best man was my cousin Andrew, who had been born in the United States in 1946. My uncle had legally adopted Andrew the day after he civilly married Mercia in 1950. When the moment came for Ken and Mercia's first holy communion in forty-three years, all of us had tears streaming down our faces. We all understood that we were celebrating forty-three years of their saying what they meant and meaning what they said. We were standing on holy ground.

DO NOT STEAL, OR ALL THE WORLD WILL DIE

In 2018 the President of the World Bank said,

> Over the last 25 years, more than a billion people have lifted themselves out of extreme poverty, and the global poverty rate is now lower than it has ever been in recorded history. This is one of the greatest human achievements of our time. But if we are going to end poverty by 2030, we need much more investment, particularly in building human capital, to help promote the inclusive growth it will take to reach the remaining poor. For their sake, we cannot fail.[3]

While this result and commitment is undeniably good, it also remains true that 17 percent of the world's population consumes 80 percent of the world's resources.

Christians have a profound obligation to share. National boundaries mean nothing to God. Given everything Jesus has to say about the rights of the poor, crippled, lame, and blind to the banquet of life, Christians are called to give priority to the needs of these members of our human family, not only because they have a just claim on our resources, but also because they can't do anything for us in return. They purify our motives. When we link our concern, time, talent, career, and money with these sisters and brothers, we tame that nagging question, "What's in it for me?" with a firm reply: "Very little—except for God's justice."

For Catholics, to share the world resources is intimately connected to the Eucharist, Christ's banquet here and now. Pedro Arrupe, former leader of the Jesuits, brought together this gift of gratitude and our mission to change the world when he said, "If there is hunger anywhere in the world, then our celebration of the Eucharist is somehow incomplete." By this he meant that when we say we are going to Mass, we are saying we are going to our commissioning to live what we have just professed. That's why some element of social justice should feature in our liturgy, especially through preaching, the prayers of the faithful, and even in the bulletin, where we may find out how we can practically apply in our daily lives what we just heard and celebrated.

This approach to the Eucharist is very traditional. St. Augustine (354–430) in his famous Easter Sermon (no. 272), said,

> If, therefore, you are the body of Christ and His members, your mystery has been placed on the Lord's Table, you receive your mystery. You reply "Amen" to that which you are, and by replying you consent. For you hear "The Body of Christ" and you reply "Amen." Be a member of the body of Christ so that your "Amen" may be true….If we receive the Eucharist worthily, we become what we receive.

Therefore, it's not just the static presence of Christ we behold, but also the challenge to share bread with the world. Deciding to use all the resources at our disposal, not only to feed the poor, but to change the international structures that keep them that way, is part of the law of love.

THE LAW OF LOVE

St. John Paul II understood this. On May 14, 1987, the pope arrived in Lima, Peru. He was met by a massive crowd of two million people. Instead of the usual greetings from the president and the cardinal, two people from a shantytown stepped forward to the microphone. Their names were Irene and Viktor Charo. As the huge crowd went quiet, they began to speak to the pope. "Holy Father, we are hungry, we are sick, we lack work, our children die before their time. Yet we believe, Holy Father, we believe in the God of life. And we hunger for bread." Before a hushed crowd, the pope replied in Spanish, "You tell me you hunger for bread." "Yes, yes," the millions yelled in reply. "You tell me you hunger for God," said the pope and again the crowd swelled with an emphatic "Yes! Yes!" "I want this hunger for God to remain; I want your hunger for bread to be satisfied." The pope then turned to the generals and the wealthy politicians gathered there—many of them devout Catholics—and said very starkly, "I won't simply say share what you have. I will say give it back. Give it back—it belongs to the poor."

HONOR OTHERS, THEIR FRAILTIES ARE USUALLY YOUR OWN

Have you noticed how many books, TV shows, films, and social media sites are about revenge and retribution? Sadly, this trend has some support in the Old Testament. Exodus 21:23–24 calls for a "life for life, eye for eye, tooth for tooth, hand for hand, foot for foot." It is also repeated in the Books of Leviticus and Deuteronomy. It has come to be called the law of retribution. And as barbaric as this law sounds to us today, in its time it was a moderating influence in society. It's clear now that in ancient Israel, before any courts were set up, personal justice could entail taking several lives for one life or torching a house for the theft of a sheep. Curiously, we have little evidence of the latter part of the law regarding eyes, teeth, and hands ever being enforced. The Israelites knew that these were figures of speech used to amplify a point. The law of retribution established the rights of courts to moderate an overly vengeful response to crime.

Jesus inherited this tradition, but clearly makes a break with it, and that's where we stand. He challenges us go against the most seductive and primitive part of our human nature, the desire to get even, because we are called to love our enemies and pray for those who persecute us. It applies to the relative we won't speak to, the former spouse against whom we poison our children, the neighbor we delight in annoying, and the work colleague we badmouth because they got the promotion we were after. That's on the domestic front. It also applies to those who commit criminal acts against us or others and the enemies of our state. This is why the Church takes a stand against the death penalty and unjust wars. And the amazing thing is that revenge and retribution have a similar effect on the domestic, national, and international scene—they solve nothing. It just eats us up. For the fleeting satisfaction revenge might bring us, it usually continues the conflict, inflames the anger, and distorts us into something much less than God intended.

Jesus does not tell us that there is no place for criticism, challenge, confrontation, and correction in the Christian life, but that we have the responsibility to be very careful about what we say about others and how we criticize and condemn them. Jesus reminds us that most of our condemnation of others is what we now call "projection," where we ignore similar failings in ourselves but roundly condemn them in others.

I think the greatest way to honor someone else is to try and always start with compassion—as Jesus does toward us. That doesn't mean we have to abandon our principles and beliefs. It means that when we judge the world, we should pray to see it as God sees it. Compassion also asks everyone in the Church to imagine in prayer what it's like to be a person of color, a refugee, a victim of domestic violence, gay, lesbian, or transgendered, divorced and remarried, or disabled. In our mission to set others free, when we catch ourselves jumping to an immediate condemnation of someone, let's stop and pray that our first response might be, "What must life be like for you?" At that point, our position is always honorable, recognizing our own frailties and touching on the Divine.

BE KIND, BE GENEROUS, AND DON'T SLEEP AROUND

The film *The Pianist* won Best Picture at the 2003 Oscars. It is the true story of Wladyslaw Szpilman, who was a celebrated classical pianist in Warsaw during the 1930s. He came from an affluent and intellectual family. Like all Jews of Warsaw, in November 1940 the Szpilmans were herded into the Jewish Ghetto. Unlike most of the others, Wladyslaw came out each day to work as a cocktail pianist in a Warsaw café. Polish Jews and Christians remembered and admired his playing, so much so that in the summer of 1942, when the rest of his family were deported to Treblinka, Wladyslaw was rescued from the train by a Jewish collaborator. The Polish resistance hid him in Warsaw. When his whereabouts were discovered, Wladyslaw went on the run and survived in a city that barely made it through the war.

Toward the end of the film there is a magnificent scene where a Nazi army officer catches the now-skeletal Wladyslaw hiding in one of the few houses left standing in Warsaw. He asks

Szpilman what he did for a living and then invites him to play the piano in the drawing room of the house. Amid the almost-total destruction of the world around them, Wladyslaw enables beauty to have the last word over the horror of war. It changes both men. It's the first time the pianist has played in years, and his concerto touches something human in the German soldier, which leads him to offer Wladyslaw his protection.

The reign of God regularly breaks in upon us. Wladyslaw's playing shows how music can do it. We believe that every day more good is done in the world than evil, or this world would destroy itself. And we hold that the source of all love is Christ. So every time we are kind rather than cruel, patient rather than intolerant, generous rather than selfish, beautiful rather than ugly, the reign of God bursts into our lives.

I consider the virtue of kindness to be one of the most underrated in the Christian life. Imagine if our first instinct was to always ask, Is what I am about to say kind? How could I make it more so? Is what I am about to do a kind thing to do? How could I make it more so? If we all lived like this, we would change the world for the better. Just as the beauty of Wladyslaw's piano cut through horror and enabled humanity to flourish, kindness does the same. It changes lives and it transform situations.

Jill E. Penley captures what acts of kindness look like:

- God won't ask what kind of car you drove, but how many people you drove who didn't have transportation.
- God won't ask the square footage of your house, but how many people you welcomed into your home.
- God won't ask about the clothes you had in your closet, but how many you helped to clothe.

THE LAW OF LOVE

- God won't ask what your highest salary was, but if you compromised your character to obtain it.
- God won't ask what your job title was, but if you performed your job to the best of your ability and with honesty and integrity.
- God won't ask how many friends you had, but how many people to whom you were a friend.
- God won't ask in what neighborhood you lived, but how you treated your neighbors.
- God won't ask about the color of your skin, but about the content of your character.[4]

We are generous simply because God has been so extravagant toward us. In fact, anything we can do for others is totally disproportionate to the gifts we have been given. Holding, as we do, that life, creation, all talents and, in our case, security and peace are fruits of God's love, then the ledger is completely tilted to the divine side. Our generosity is not just about money we may share but being generous with our time, talent, hospitality, and compassion, even with our praise of other people. Often the people we find it hardest to praise are the ones to whom we are closest, our wife or husband, children, friends, parents, or members of religious communities. Our generosity finds opportunities to truly and authentically celebrate what we can.

The final part of the original commandments hinges on the word *covet*, which means to wrongfully desire something or someone without due regard for the rights of the other or the consequences of acting upon our desire. Appleyard says, "Don't sleep around." When it comes to sexuality we give such mixed messages to the next generation that we cannot be surprised when others have distorted views about recognizing healthy desires, self-control, and seeing the potential hurt that can come from making poor choices. In an oversexualized culture, pornography is now an identifiable and treatable addiction. On one hand, we say that sex is just one of many recreational options that can be enjoyed even if devoid of relationships, trust, and dignity; and yet on the other, we have all seen the carnage in committed relationships when people cannot settle into monogamy because they really never have, and society no longer values and supports it as it once did.

For many years I have assisted couples as they prepare for marriage. I use a resource that has questions for them to think about and discuss in between sessions. One of the questions at the end of one of the chapters is, "What effect would *adultery* have on your marriage?" In one sense this hypothetical question is absurd. Dealing with the consequences of any sin requires time and place, context and contrition. It is even tougher to imagine the effect of any destructive behavior in one's marriage even before the marriage has begun. Still, it never ceases to amaze me how this question usually leads the couple to have a very fruitful and frank discussion, not about adultery, but about their values, family history, commitment, fidelity, and growing old together. Sometimes, however, I cringe when the prospective bride or groom seems to give the green light to their future spouse by saying, "Well I guess if he or she went looking elsewhere it would be my fault," or "I love him or her so much that I know we could go on regardless." Others say very clearly that it would alter the trust and respect of the relationship, but they hope they could look at the circumstances and rebuild the relationship. The most mature couples do not weep over the seriousness of "sleeping around," but want to hold on to compassion, forgiveness, and a commitment that it will not happen again.

What this commandment establishes is that we all need boundaries, and the body is the point of commitment. We can say we love people forever, but if we sleep around, our body is telling another story. We have been told a lie. Sex is not another recreational option. It is a way of embodying the call of love, to be kind and generous. Before we act on our desire to sleep around, that would be the perfect time to ask whether this is the kindest thing I can do to the one I love and to myself right now.

By putting some ancient words into the modern vernacular, we are exhorted to seriousness, facing reality, humility, creating space, respecting age, honesty, and fidelity, and we are bluntly told to stop killing, stealing, and sleeping around. The wisdom of these values is the basis of love and means we are not yet done with the Ten Commandments, and they are not yet done with us.

CHAPTER 3

THE BEATITUDES
(or the Sermon on the Mount or on the Plain)

When Jesus saw the crowds, he went up the mountain; and after he sat down, his disciples came to him. Then he began to speak, and taught them, saying:

"Blessed are the poor in spirit, for theirs is the kingdom of heaven.

"Blessed are those who mourn, for they will be comforted.

"Blessed are the meek, for they will inherit the earth.

"Blessed are those who hunger and thirst for righteousness, for they will be filled.

"Blessed are the merciful, for they will receive mercy.

"Blessed are the pure in heart, for they will see God.

"Blessed are the peacemakers, for they will be called children of God.

"Blessed are those who are persecuted for righteousness' sake, for theirs is the kingdom of heaven.

THE LAW OF LOVE

"Blessed are you when people revile you and persecute you and utter all kinds of evil against you falsely on my account. Rejoice and be glad, for your reward is great in heaven, for in the same way they persecuted the prophets who were before you."

(Matt 5:1–11)

In any walk of life there are stories that circulate about an important facet of your job. For priests, these stories often focus on sermons. A young priest was having trouble with his sermons, so he asked the bishop for help. "Well," said the bishop, "you might start with something to get the congregation's attention, such as, 'Last night I was in the warm embrace of a good woman.' I've always found that sparks their interest and then you can go on to talk about how warm and accepting she was and at the end reveal she was your mother. It's great for sermons about family love."

The young priest decided to take the advice the following Sunday, but he was so nervous, something got lost in the translation. He started, "Last night I was in the arms of a hot woman." As the congregation audibly gasped, the young priest paused and realized he had forgotten how the bishop's story ended, so he said, "I don't remember who she was, but the bishop recommended her."

Whether it happened on the mount (Matthew) or on the plain (Luke), this Sermon is one of the greatest homilies ever given. What makes it great is not just the beauty of its language or the hope of its theology. It is truly great because Jesus was preaching to the reality in front of him. The Jews of Israel listening that day were poor, grieving, meek, and hungry for justice. Some were trying to be merciful to their enemies, struggling to find God amid persecution and attempting to make peace while their family and friends were being falsely accused and condemned. As true as this was for the Jews of Jesus's day, it was even more so for the earliest Christian community for whom this Gospel was written.

Sometimes when we hear a sermon our reaction can be, "What would he or she know of the complexities of my life? If they did, they would soon change their tune!" When, in the Sermon on the Mount, Jesus says, "Blessed are those" he is not being patronizing, glossing over all sorts of tough human realities with, "Well done, keep it up, be happy, and we'll fix it all up in heaven."

First, some history. The word for blessing in New Testament Greek is *makarios*. It is used twenty-six times in the New Testament: ten times in Matthew's Gospel, nine times in his Beatitudes, and in Matthew 13:16; and eight times in Luke, six in his Beatitudes, and on four other occasions. The Old Testament word for a blessing is *berakhah*, which in Hebrew can mean "on bended knee," as in thanksgiving to God. It can also mean to be "on the lap," as in a child climbing into the lap of a trusted adult. These last two meanings would have been the meanings Jesus would have had inherited and deployed. They change the sense of a blessing from glossing over all sorts of tough human realities with, "Well done, keep it up, be happy, and we'll fix it all up in heaven," to discovering that God is present and active in one's experience, right here and right now.

This reading picks up the intimacy of a blessing as portrayed in Genesis 30:3; 48:8 and Job 3:12, where the text suggests we do not need to go past our own daily struggles to find the presence of God. Just as a child who climbs into the lap of a loving parent feels safe against the travails of life, so we can find the same reassurance and comfort with God, finding God's presence right here and now. This is a very different type of lawgiver than the one who was on Mount Sinai, handing down to Moses the Torah from on high. Here is a companionable God who preaches

49

THE LAW OF LOVE

on another mountain but is given to us as our brother, walking beside us as we get out of bed and meet the days we would rather not face. Jesus teaches us that God is not impervious to our pain and happiness, or a great manipulator desiring terrible things to punish us or teach us something. The God of the Beatitudes is the one to whom we bend the knee of gratitude toward because he is utterly committed to our human adventure as one with us, in our flesh, as God's body language.

The image of God that emerges in the Beatitudes is not the classic lawgiver as much as the friend who enables us to find meaning and hope in struggles of our lives. Sadly, God-as-friend is a rich image not used as much as it should be. We choose our friends, we like to spend time with them, and we tell our intimate friends things we tell few others. Sometimes, when we are on top of the world or in a crisis, we call our best friends ahead of our family. And we know our friends like us because they seek us out and want to share our life. Jesus used the analogy of friendship when referring to the relationship he wanted to have with us, and so we can claim he is the best friend we can ever have, interested in every daily event; he's there for us at every moment in life. Yet he doesn't barge in. He waits patiently for an invitation to enter our lives at whatever level we want. Jesus-as-friend doesn't give us old-fashioned sermons, but rather meets us where we are, embraces us and holds us close when the going gets tough, and helps us find the way forward. Jesus-as-friend is the greatest Beatitude of all.

I want to explore Matthew's Beatitudes more than Luke's because they seem to be modeled on the Ten Commandments but depart in vital ways. Both are given to crowds who have been traveling and are given on mountains. One has ten laws, the other has nine affirmations. The tenth clause in Matthew's Beatitudes is a statement of encouragement: "Rejoice and be glad, for your reward is great in heaven, for in the same way they persecuted the prophets who were before you" (Matt 5:12). Both set an agenda for the Israelites, with one becoming the core expression of the Torah, and the other expressing many of the key messages Jesus addresses through Matthew's Gospel. Both communications attend to ethical living and carry within them tensions between the personal and the public, the present and hereafter.

In context, Jesus is interpreting the law by recrafting it in the Beatitudes. This becomes explicit in what follows (Matt 5:21–48) where Jesus explicitly lays out, "You have heard that it was said to those of ancient times" regarding murder, judgment, adultery, divorce, oaths, revenge, and loving our neighbor and hating our enemy, followed by, "But I say to you...." Jesus, the new Moses, the fulfillment of all the prophets longed to see, takes the Torah and refashions it into a way of discovering that God is present and active in one's experience, right here and right now.

Moses is explicitly given the law by God, and Jesus directly addresses the law in Matthew 5:17–19:

> Do not think that I have come to abolish the law or the prophets; I have come not to abolish but to fulfill. For truly I tell you, until heaven and earth pass away, not one letter, not one stroke of a letter, will pass from the law until all is accomplished. Therefore, whoever breaks one of the least of these commandments, and teaches others to do the same, will be called least in the kingdom of heaven; but whoever does them and teaches them will be called great in the kingdom of heaven.

Not only do the Beatitudes tell us that when we are poor, compassionate, mournful, campaigning for a just society and suffering because of it, gentle, innocent, making peace, and being martyred, we are encountering the presence of God in a special way, but they also establish the way of seeing these things in a contemporary context.

Pope Francis did exactly that with his six "modern Beatitudes" that he proposed at Malmö, Sweden, on All Saints Day 2016:

- Blessed are those who remain faithful while enduring evils inflicted on them by others and forgive them from their heart.
- Blessed are those who look into the eyes of the abandoned and marginalized and show them their closeness.
- Blessed are those who see God in every person and strive to make others also discover him.
- Blessed are those who protect and care for our common home.
- Blessed are those who renounce their own comfort in order to help others.
- Blessed are those who pray and work for full communion between Christians.

Taking the pope's lead, here are nine modern ways we can be consoled and challenged by the Beatitudes, so that we avoid evil and live the law of love.

BLESSED ARE THE POOR IN SPIRIT, FOR THEIRS IS THE KINGDOM OF HEAVEN

Luke puts this first Beatitude more bluntly: "Blessed are the poor." Some argue that Matthew softens the challenge of standing with the economically poor by adding "in spirit." I am not convinced by those arguments. There are two words used for the poor in the Gospels: *penas*, which refers to physical laborers, and *ptochos*, which means "beggar." Both Luke and Matthew use the latter term, which has a direct association with the economically poor: "blessed are you who are beggars" highlights how we are all beggars in the life of grace. We cannot buy, earn, or demand our invitation into the family of God. It is a free, undeserved, and unwarranted invitation, offered to the rich and poor alike. Our humanity, including that of our spirit, leaves us bereft of the hope and meaning we need to exist, until we search for, are invited into, and discover the reign of God wherein we flourish.

I think one of the best examples of those who are begging for hope and justice in the Christian family right now are the survivors of sexual abuse by Church personnel. When they sought the truth, they were told they were liars. They have spoken truth to power when power discounted their testimony. And with grace working in and through them, they are some of the most important and necessary truth-tellers in the life of the Church.

For those of us who have met survivors of clerical sexual abuse of minors, and the secondary victims, their families, we know that no apology can ever repair the damage, no amount of compensation can give someone back their innocence and childhood, and no act of reparation or penance can ever adequately express the shame and sorrow of what all of us feel over what a very few clergy have done. Adding to their pain has been the despicable cover-up of these heinous crimes at every level and layer of the Church.

Our present-day beggars in spirit lead us to the kingdom of heaven through true repentance and reconciliation. This starts with telling the truth, no matter how painful it is to say it or hear it, especially when it involves institutional and generational cover-up. They are speaking for other survivors, their families and friends, and for the dead whose trauma became too much. A raw and painful sign of God's solidarity with us now is hearing the cry of the poor who are begging for truth and justice, which Jesus says are among the greatest signs of the kingdom of heaven.

BLESSED ARE THOSE WHO MOURN, FOR THEY WILL BE COMFORTED

When we hear the mistranslation of the word *blessed* as "happy are those who mourn," we can see how this Beatitude seems to have inherent contradictions. As we have seen, we are not being called to be "happy" in sadness, but to find God amid our grief and pain.

The often unacknowledged Old Testament background to this idea is critical to a new reading of it and its contemporary call to love. In the Old Testament and especially in the Psalms, the people of Israel had no problem inviting God into their personal, communal, and liturgical laments, an expression of pain, crying to God about how they were experiencing their present lives and inviting God into the griefs and anxieties of the moment. I think many Christians have lost the power of lamentation.

In the Psalms the authors cry, scream, demand, and rail against God over their pain. Of the 150 psalms we have, 65 are categorized as cries of lament, anger, protest, despair, and complaint. Some of them are sometimes called the "cursing psalms." Psalm 88, the darkest of all the Psalms, and Psalms 3, 12, 22, 44, 57, 80, and 139 are good examples of calling on God to be present in grief and pain. Not that I share in any way the Psalmist's belief that God has sent the misfortune in an active way, but I am in awe of the way the Psalmist unloads on God. It is consoling. Such confidence. God has big shoulders and therefore understands our lamentations because he knows the anguish in our hearts. I think God lives by the generally sensible advice: better out than in. Our comfort in our grief starts with bothering God a lot more with our lamentations. We do not have to be so tame.

As we have seen, prescientific religious people gave everything they did not understand a theological reading. Floods, famines, and plagues, physical diseases and illnesses were intended by God to punish, warn, or teach his chosen people. The Book of Job is the best example of a theology that sees personal and physical suffering as God-given. As poetic and moving as that book is, it is also a profound lament exploring heartbreaking theology. The New Testament authors are of two minds about the sources of human suffering. In some instances, Jesus tells people not to sin again so that they will avoid future illnesses (John 5:14), and on other occasions he rejects personal or family sinfulness as the cause for personal suffering, as in Luke 13:4: "Or those eighteen who were killed when the tower of Siloam fell on them—do you think that they were worse offenders than all the others living in Jerusalem?" What we do know is that in every Gospel Jesus is always moved to compassion by the person in front of him and he tries to restore them physically, socially, and spiritually (Mark 1:40–45; 9:14–29).

As Christians we know that love took human form in Jesus Christ, and so we have a God who not only entered into our life, but also was subjected to and embraced the alienation of grief, pain, suffering, and death. We are the only world religion to believe that. Johannes B. Metz in *Poverty of Spirit* summarized it perfectly:

> Jesus did not cling to his divinity. He did not simply dip into our existence, wave the magic wand of divine life over us, and then hurriedly retreat to his eternal home.

He did not leave us with a tattered dream, letting us brood over the mystery of our existence. Instead, Jesus subjected himself to our plight. He immersed himself in our misery and followed man's [sic] road to the end. He did not escape from the torment of our life, nobly repudiating man. With the full weight of his divinity he descended into the abyss of human existence, penetrating its darkest depths. He was not spared from the dark mystery of our poverty as human beings.[1]

Jesus's full and true divinity cannot obliterate his humanity, or he would be play-acting at being human. His tears at Lazarus's tomb and crying over Jerusalem were real. Christ came to "comfort the afflicted and afflict the comfortable." We need both and maybe the kingdom of heaven is found in the tension between the two.

BLESSED ARE THE MEEK, FOR THEY WILL INHERIT THE EARTH

The only contemporary setting in which we talk about people being meek is to say someone is "meek and mild." If we describe someone as meek, on its own, it is not usually positive but implies the person can't stand up for him- or herself. I have always associated the term with being an introvert, and in this regard, Jesus seems to endorse that those who are to inherit his kingdom are those who are lower key and reserved. My problem is that I am an extrovert and I have always believed that most of the Church's traditions and prayer practices seemed to be "the revenge of introverts" on the other half of humanity. I do not doubt for a moment the value of an hour's meditation with a straight back, regulating breathing, hands in one's lap, or, even worse, sitting on a prayer stool. It's just that these venerable styles of prayer are easier for introverts than for those of us who are more outgoing and look to stimulation from external things or objective considerations. Retreat days, weeks, or the thirty-day retreat, as much as I now relish them, seemed to me to be delicious forms of torture from the spiritually introverted, who have had the upper hand in our tradition for a very long time. The meek have well and truly inherited Christian spirituality and made the rest of us feel guilty.

However, in the ancient world *meek* did not mean introverted, passive, or shy. In Greek, the word Matthew uses for meek is *praus*. It is argued that the term came into general usage from the military. Xenophon, in *The Art of Horsemanship*, says *praus* relates to horse training:

> The Greek army would find the wildest horses in the mountains and bring them to be broken in. After months of training they sorted the horses into categories: some were discarded, some broken and made useful for bearing burdens, some were useful for ordinary duty and the fewest of all graduated as war horses. When a horse passed the conditioning required for a war horse, its state was described as "praus." The war horse had "power under authority," "strength under control." A war horse never ceased to be determined, strong and passionate. However, it learned to bring its nature under discipline. It gave up being wild, unruly, out of control and rebellious. A war horse learned to bring that nature under control. It would now respond to the slightest touch of the rider, stand in the face of cannon fire, thunder into battle and stop at a whisper. It was now praus, meek.[2]

THE LAW OF LOVE

In Jesus's time, a meek person was one who could have been as bold and extroverted as nature dictated but was open to grace building on that nature in and through their formation in Christ. The meek can be forceful and determined but obedient to God's law of love. The meek inherit the kingdom of God not because they are pushovers but because they have the humility to submit to a greater cause, a higher power, and to discipline. For Jesus, the meek were the team players, using their gifts and talents, not for self-aggrandizement, but with the self-restraint needed to serve the reign of God. The meek are selected from the pack because they have learned the art and practice of obedience.

Obedience is not about hearing "jump" and asking "how high?" That's infantile subservience. Christian obedience is richer than that. The word *obedience* comes from the Latin word *obedire*, meaning "to listen." If we all want to be obedient to God's reign in our world and lives, we better become good at listening in all its forms, because we believe that God listens to and hears us. The meek are humble enough to take wise advice wisely. We are not meant to be "rocks and islands," operating on our own. We need the wisdom of our families and most trusted friends, the Church, and sometimes professionals to inform our consciences, make the best possible decisions before God, and then have the self-insight and restraint to respond to the promptings of the Holy Spirit as we engage in the battle between good and evil.

BLESSED ARE THOSE WHO HUNGER AND THIRST FOR RIGHTEOUSNESS, FOR THEY WILL BE FILLED

Interpretation of this Beatitude often and understandably focuses on being "righteous." It's an unfortunate word for modern ears because it is generally associated with being inflexible, condemning, or dismissing others who do not share our ideology or practice. Other synonyms for *righteousness* help unpack what it means in better contemporary language: ethical, good, honest, honorable, or one who practices what he or she preaches. Rather than just focus on the righteousness to which Jesus calls us, I think we should take the other verbs around it just as seriously: hunger, thirst, and being filled. These four words indicate what we should be righteous about. This trio of actions is often associated with those in our world who have nothing. This Beatitude calls us to practice what we preach about filling up the hungry and quenching the thirst of those who are parched.

In recent decades we have rightly emphasized the love and compassion of Jesus because in centuries past the steadfast love of Christ was underemphasized. We should never think, however, that it cancels out the anger God feels when he sees an unjust world filled with people who know better and do nothing. In the Bible we hear about righteous anger, where God or humanity realizes something is so wrong that "holy anger" is the first and right response. At its best in the Scriptures, this anger leads to justice, to making things right. It is the moment of realization where we can become as "mad as hell" and "not take this anymore" and enable holy, righteous anger to demand change. This is the start of finding God's blessing in filling the hungry.

John F. Kennedy said in his address to the UN General Assembly on September 20, 1963, "Never before has man [*sic*] had such capacity to control his own environment, to end thirst and hunger, to conquer poverty and disease, to banish illiteracy and massive human misery. We have the power to make this the best generation of mankind in the history of the world—or to make it the last." We could feed the world's poor. We choose not to. UNICEF estimates that sixteen thousand children die each day from starvation. That means eleven children die every minute of every day. The UN's Food and Agriculture Organization says that general poverty, lack of democracy, civil war, and unjust access to world markets are as much to blame for starvation as climatic factors, if not more so now. So when people say, "Why does God let famine and starvation happen?" I imagine God shaking his head in tearful reply, "Why do *you* let famine and starvation happen?"

God becomes a convenient whipping boy at this point, but the ball is squarely in our court. In a world where all people could be fed, why do people starve? We choose it to be this way. Indeed, some frustrated economists who work in this area go as far as to say the G20 needs it this way and structures the global market accordingly. Whatever the details, the evil here is ours, and God will call us to account for it. And because of access to all forms of media, we will not be able to say to God that we did not know either the scale of the problem or our complicity within it. Ignorance cannot be our defense. The same is true of other examples as well: environmental degradation, personal and social stress, and lack of action to end war. We choose the world to be like this, and then blame God for the negative fallout from our decisions.

If we are going to be blessed practicing what we preach regarding feeding and filling God's children who have nothing, I think it starts at the family dining room table. As a priest I often have the great honor of being invited into people's homes for a family meal. It's almost always a very enjoyable experience. Mind you, things have changed in many homes and, these days, on arrival at the table, when I am invited to say grace before meals, an assertive adolescent says, "Why are we saying grace? We never say grace! Why are you playing it up for the priest?" To which I reply, "We're saying grace because sixteen thousand kids your age or younger will die today from starvation. So we take one moment to be grateful for the food we have, and the strength it gives us to make the world a more just place for every-one." I have never actually said that, but I really want to!

St. Augustine, in a sermon on August 9, 413, wrote that the Eucharist was about three things: goodness, unity, and charity. Augustine taught that if we were not better people, working for unity and loving each other away from the Eucharist, it fails to achieve its purpose. The blessing of being ethical, good, honest, and honorable rises and falls on us linking the reception of the Bread of Life at the Eucharist with the giving of bread that sustains life away from it, so that we see to it that not one of the thirty thousand children of God who still die every day in our world would have to.

BLESSED ARE THE MERCIFUL, FOR THEY WILL RECEIVE MERCY

If ever a Beatitude was to have a patron saint, then Pope Francis must be this one's. On March 13, 2015, the pope announced that there would be an extraordinary Jubilee Year from December 8, 2015 (the Third Sunday of Advent, Gaudete or "Rejoicing" Sunday and the Feast of the Immaculate Conception) to November 20, 2016 (the Feast of Christ the King). Jubilee Years were instituted by Pope Boniface VIII in 1300, initially to be observed every hundred years to celebrate God's forgiveness of our sins. The hundred-year tradition was amended in the four-teenth century by Pope Clement VI to hold them every fifty years. Pope John Paul II broke the fifty years tradition with a special one in 1983 celebrating our redemption in Christ.

The whole idea of a jubilee as we celebrate it today comes from the Old Testament. The root of the word is from the Hebrew *yobhel*, which refers to the ram's horn that sounded all over Israel to usher in a Jubilee Year. In biblical times, most people were dead by age fifty, so a Jubilee Year was a once-in-a-lifetime event often marked by three major events: slaves were set free, the fields were allowed to go fallow for a year, and debts were forgiven.

These elements can have a modern application. For example, in facing the crucible of the sexual abuse crisis recently, the whole Church has been set free from misplaced loyalty to the institution and a renewed commitment to truth, transparency, justice, and love. The outcome of the fields left fallow was that the regenerated soil brought forth an even greater harvest. As we have already seen, Pope Francis has also placed the care of creation at the center of his papacy, as the great right-to-life issue of our time. And then to the forgiveness of debts.

The word *mercy*, though biblically rich, can be, at least in English, an unfortunate word. When we talk of law courts or people being merciful, and though it is entirely admirable, it indicates a one-way relationship, a powerful person or institution bestowing an outpouring of goodness on the recipient. Perfect for our relationship with God, but it does not capture the relationship and mutuality inherent in the action. The words *compassion* and *forgiveness* make a much stronger claim on our behavior. Maybe a Year of Compassion might have caught our imaginations even more.

Whatever word the pope did or didn't use, in a world hell-bent on retribution and revenge, it was inspired of Francis to call us to be our best Christian selves, forgiving as we have been forgiven. Reflect on what the pope said throughout the Jubilee Year, which puts practical action around this Beatitude.

- "The Lord never tires of forgiving. It is we who tire of asking for forgiveness."

- "A little bit of mercy makes the world less cold and more just."
- "Too often we participate in the globalization of indifference. May we strive instead to live global solidarity."
- "Small gestures of love, of tenderness, of care, make people feel that the Lord is with us. This is how the door of mercy opens. God has caressed us with his mercy. Let us bring God's tender caress to others, to those who are in need."
- "The way of the Church is not to condemn anyone forever, it is to pour out the balm of God's mercy."
- "With the weapons of love, God has defeated selfishness and death. His Son Jesus is the door of mercy wide open to all."
- "To be merciful means to grow in a love that is courageous, generous and real."
- "In a broken world, to communicate with mercy means to help create closeness between the children of God."
- "The tenderness of God is present in the lives of all those who attend the sick and understand their needs, with eyes full of love."
- "The time has come for the Church to take up the joyful call to mercy once more. It is time to return to the basics and to bear the weaknesses and struggles of our brothers and sisters.",
- "If I had to sum it up in one word I would say that mercy is about being large-hearted. Our God is a large-hearted God."
- "If up till now you have kept him at a distance, step forward. He will receive you with open arms."

THE LAW OF LOVE

- "Jesus affirms that mercy is not only an action of the Father, it becomes a criterion for ascertaining who his true children are. In short, we are called to show mercy because mercy has first been shown to us."
- "Pardoning offences becomes the clearest expression of merciful love, and for us Christians it is an imperative from which we cannot excuse ourselves."
- "I think we too are the people who, on the one hand, want to listen to Jesus, but on the other hand, at times, like to find a stick to beat others with, to condemn others. And Jesus has this message for us: mercy. That this is the Lord's most powerful message: mercy."

By the end of the Year of Mercy, Pope Francis was challenging us to make sure that the first words we use when we speak to one another and to the world should not be words of condemnation but words of love, compassion, and mercy. "The good shepherd was not ashamed of touching the wounded flesh. Let us not forget this: The good shepherd is always close to the people, always, as God our father has made himself close to us in Jesus Christ made flesh." Therefore, the blessing of being a compassionate person is to the degree we recognize the gift and giver of being forgiven by God.

Don't tell some Christians this, but Jesus says next to nothing about sex in the Gospels. That doesn't mean it's not important. It is just a fact that he very rarely addressed himself to sexuality in either a positive or negative way. Maybe he knew some theologians weren't going to shut up about it for the next two thousand years! According to the Gospels, the two biggest sins Jesus returns to the most are hypocrisy—all of us at some point say one thing and do another—and those who will not forgive. Indeed, it is easy to see how hypocrisy and forgiveness are linked. In the mind of Jesus maybe the greatest betrayal is telling others that they should forgive those who have hurt them, and then not practicing what we preach by forgiving others ourselves. Could it be said of us at our Christian burial, "Here, we bid farewell to a merciful person"? Potentially, that could be the greatest thing ever said of a follower of Jesus Christ.

BLESSED ARE THE PURE IN HEART, FOR THEY WILL SEE GOD

On first reading, this Beatitude appears to be one for very few people. Even though we all long to see God, few of us are "pure in heart." Most of us are a mixed bag of mixed motivations. In fact, St. Ignatius Loyola said the art of spiritual discernment was to purify our desires and align them more with God's desires for the world.

By definition, saints are saints because they see God, and fortunately for us, some of the saints needed a lot of purification of their hearts to get there. Two of the earliest and most important Christian saints prove how complex and blessed the road to seeing God through purity of heart can be: Sts. Peter and Paul. Though both were crucial to the early Christian community's survival and expansion, their worst moments may have the most to teach us right now.

Peter's infamous denial gives comfort to any of us who ever in a moment of weakness chose self-preservation over faithfulness. This uneducated, brash, and impulsive man was in the end to give the greatest witness to faith in Christ, but it came through

THE LAW OF LOVE

the tears of having betrayed—not once but three times—the one who had loved him and who had called him his "rock." Even after having been forgiven and having assumed the leadership of the nascent Church, Peter still does not seem to get who Christ's kingdom is for—everyone. When it came to preaching the gospel to the Gentiles and to adapting the demands of the Jewish law to new Christians, Peter was late to the party. But he was humble enough to admit he was wrong. In the end, he got with the program. He ended up dying for it.

Paul is an even more complex character. Every time I have heard about religious fanatics doing murderous things in God's name, I think of St. Paul. We have conveniently whitewashed his story. Paul may have been a highly educated tentmaker, but he was early on also a religious fruitcake—a murderous zealot. From Acts 9, Philippians, and Galatians, and to a lesser degree 1 Timothy and 1 Corinthians, we know that this self-confessed "chief among the sinners" went from town to town presiding over the extermination of Christians. No wonder the earliest disciples were wary of him and of his dramatic conversion from being an extreme Jewish nationalist to the greatest of Christian missionaries.

In both Peter and Paul, but in different and equally rewarding ways, we can celebrate the truth of that old dictum: "It doesn't matter where you start, but where you finish." Rather than sanitize their stories of failure and brutality, I find comfort in their warts-and-all histories, which eventually end in giving glory to him whose power working in them could do infinitely more than they could ever ask or imagine. It also puts paid to the idea that the Church has ever been a community of the simply pure of heart, but more that our hearts of flesh started out as hearts of stone. Peter and Paul were loved sinners whose conversions to Christ were hard-won and took time. Just like us.

Because the people of the ancient world could feel their hearts beat, and see it move, and they knew that when it stopped people died, then they believed that the heart rather than the brain controlled the body. Understandably in this prescientific world the heart was given mystical properties. Even today we still talk about people who have "big, good, or full hearts," are "warm or broken hearted," or are "heartless." These metaphorical uses of the word point to a presence or an absence of love. And the best continuing example of this tradition is St. Valentine's Day, an obscure Roman martyr, whose feast day took over a pagan festival of love. It's not by accident that February 14 is covered in hearts.

In calling us to purity in heart Jesus no doubt was invoking 1 Samuel 16:7: "Do not look on his appearance or on the height of his stature, because I have rejected him; for the LORD does not see as mortals see; they look on the outward appearance, but the LORD looks on the heart." This is confirmed when later in Matthew's Gospel, in the opposite of the Beatitudes—the "woes and betides"—Jesus confronts his opponents. "Woe to you, scribes and Pharisees, hypocrites! For you clean the outside of the cup and of the plate, but inside they are full of greed and self-indulgence. You blind Pharisee! First clean the inside of the cup, so that the outside also may become clean" (Matt 23:25–26).

Those who will see God have purified hearts because they have stopped putting on a show for God or for the world and live lives that authentically reflect the heart of Christ: Jesus's humanity is celebrated; his suffering and death is seen as an expression of his love for us, and the Eucharist is the most intimate of moments where Christ is broken; we are poured out in love so that we can reproduce the pattern of his sacrificial love in our own lives; and we are drawn by love rather than being driven by fear. Saints

Peter and Paul are proof positive that this is the great promise to which we are called.

BLESSED ARE THE PEACEMAKERS, FOR THEY WILL BE CALLED CHILDREN OF GOD

Is it a coincidence that the Beatitude about peace is the seventh one, the perfect number? More in a moment on how peace is the great gift Christ brings his disciples, but for now we have to deal with the seeming contradiction between this Beatitude in Matthew 5:9 and Matthew 10:34: "Do not think that I have come to bring peace to the earth; I have not come to bring peace, but a sword." The context for the latter verse is Jesus preparing his disciples for their mission and looking at the consequences that will follow: opposition and martyrdom. The sword can be read in how people responded to Christ, in division, not in advocating how the gospel should be spread. Most scholars agree Matthew's Gospel was written between AD 80 and 90, after the destruction of Jerusalem and the temple by the Romans in AD 70, and the First Jewish-Roman War, AD 66–73; the sad reality was that by that time, division, rejection, and suffering were everywhere, in families, in Judaism, and between nations. The sword was the fallout of their world falling apart, not Christ's advocacy to wield it. Matthew 10 can be read as prophecy and preparation for what is coming.

Taking Matthew and the other Gospels as a whole, Jesus advocates peace; and when Christ appears after being raised from the dead, he first bequeaths the gift of peace. It is the primary Easter gift, and yet there have been times when Christianity has been guilty of talking about peace as a spiritual wallpaper over some tough realities, rather than preaching that God's peace is our companion in facing up to whatever our reality is and dealing with it. However, peace is like all the best things in life: an attitude of mind and a habit born of consistently making good choices. Some people can do a large amount of work and be quite serene about it. Peace, for them, is a way of life, of being a contemplative in action.

In this regard I have always been touched by the opening lines of Jill Jackson-Miller and Sy Miller's 1955 song, "Let There Be Peace on Earth":

Let there be peace on earth
And let it begin with me.

We might pray for "world peace," but, like all the virtues, it begins with me being at peace. Before I presided at my first Mass of thanksgiving, an old priest gave me a great piece of advice. "Never underestimate the burdens the parishioners bring with them into the Church. Often, we have little idea of the difficulties and pain our parishioners will be carrying, and many just come along for a little bit of peace. For Christ's sake, don't add to their burdens."

Being blessed with the gift of peace first means that because we have experienced the love of God, we know we never carry our burdens alone, because Christ is our companion and guide. Jesus didn't come to us as a divine magician, waving a wand over our problems to wipe away all our tears. Rather, he enables us to see that the gift of peace is often found in having the perspective in exercising the gift of right judgment, making the best possible choices, and often the healing of memories. The Christian Church is challenged to be the place where we undertake these things, carrying each other's burdens in human solidarity.

THE LAW OF LOVE

To be blessed with peace we need to become more contemplative. Being active in our lives and engaged with the world around us is a gift, but if we are honest about our busyness, some of it is not virtuous. It's about denial, avoidance, or trying to keep up with our peer group. It's curious, isn't it, that just as we all compete to be the busiest person we know, we also complain that what we really want is "some peace and quiet"? We can't have it both ways. Compulsive frantic activity is the enemy of peace.

So while peace begins with me, it is not just about me. The other vital element in this Beatitude is that Jesus also tells us that if we want to have peace, we are going to have to work for it by resolving conflict. In 1967 St. Pope Paul VI, in his groundbreaking letter *Populorum Progressio*, said that the best path to world peace was the development of peoples in regard to just wages; security of employment; fair working conditions; respect for the universal rights of religion, speech, the press, of assembly, and to vote; a more equitable sharing of the world's resources; and an end to war.

In previous writings I have refuted the charge that is often asserted but never proven, that religion is the cause of most wars. I don't want to let my coreligionists off the hook for the criminal acts and suffering they have perpetrated upon our sisters and brothers, but any careful analysis of almost all wars bears out that religion has not been the primary cause of most wars. Certainly, religion has had and does have a role to play in the justification of war, and some shocking deeds have been done and are done in the name of God.

The reality is that religion, as one among many tools, has been and is sometimes used in political, social, and ethnic wars, in the false search for social and political uniformity and colonial dominance. Furthermore, apart from war—even more tragically—religion has mounted its own persecutions. I do not want to run away from the despicable fallout from the 595-year reign of the "inquisitors of heretical depravity." It is impossible to know how many people were killed in this period by these theological tyrants, but most reputable scholars on the Inquisition conclude that it was somewhere between three thousand and fifty thousand people. Not one person should have been murdered for who they were (homosexuals), for what they did (notorious sinners and so-called witches), and for what they believed (atheists, Jews, and Muslims). Having now formally apologized for the Inquisition (easy in hindsight), to my knowledge the Catholic Church has not sanctioned the death of anyone since 1826, which is more than we can say for any other nation or state on earth.

Despite what some contemporary atheists say, the sad reality is that most human conflict is fought over greed for land or resources, political power, and conflict over cultural, tribal, national, and social issues. Religion is one of the many things used to uphold the righteousness of the claim and the justification for war. And this Beatitude means we must do all we can to work for peace through the just claim of all God's children to the things that are universally theirs, and to the peaceful resolution of conflicts. Mixing my metaphors, peace is a double-edged sword.

> Peace looked down and saw war.
> "I will go there," said peace.
> Love looked down and saw hatred.
> "I will go there," said love.
> So he,
> the Lord of Light,
> the Prince of Peace,
> the King of Love,
> came down and crept in beside us.[3]

THE LAW OF LOVE

While every one of the Beatitudes has personal and social dimensions to them, the seventh has more claim on us in this regard than the others. Maybe that's why the order of the Beatitudes may not be a coincidence, because being a person of peace is about God creating us as such and then continually recreating us so that we resolve conflict nonviolently every time.

BLESSED ARE THOSE WHO ARE PERSECUTED FOR RIGHTEOUSNESS' SAKE, FOR THEIRS IS THE KINGDOM OF HEAVEN

The first people honored by the earliest Christians, the first saints, were the martyrs, those who lived out the eighth Beatitude to its tragic conclusion in giving their lives for Christ. The word *martyr* comes from the word *witness*. In fact, All Saints Day, celebrated throughout the Church on November 1st, has its roots in the early Church's "Martyrs Day," attested to by a hymn written in 359 by St. Ephraim. The name was changed to All Saints Day in the seventh century.

Our faith is built upon the witness of the martyrs. Our Christian foremothers and forefathers counted themselves blessed to suffer and die as Jesus suffered and died. They lived out the words in John's Gospel: "I tell you, unless a grain of wheat falls into the earth and dies, it remains just a single grain; but if it dies, it bears much fruit. Those who love their life lose it, and those who hate their life in this world will keep it for eternal life" (John 12:24–25). Indeed, the presence of godparents at baptism comes from the time of Christian persecution. Christians, who had left their Jewish or Gentile families to join the Christian community, had to confront the fact that they could be martyred for their faith. If they were killed, they did not want their children to return to their non-Christian extended families. In this context, they asked other Christians in God's name to swear they would take their children into their homes and raise them as their own, becoming their mother or father. A godparent was honored to raise the children of those persecuted for the kingdom of heaven. Prophets and martyrs are often linked. They are put to death because they cannot live any other way. Such is the liberty of spirit, thirst for justice, and witness to truth they embody, that they so threaten the social and religious leaders of their time and place that they must be silenced.

The problem with glorifying suffering and martyrdom in any context is that this can attract fanatics. As uncomfortable as it is for Christians to admit, some of our martyrs did not die with the healthiest of religious motivations. We have only to read their letters to discover that they actively went looking for death, longing and praying that "the crown of martyrdom" would be granted to them. Paradise awaited. While it's all good and well for comfortable believers like me to be critical of those who sacrificed their lives, there is an important distinction to be made between being killed as a result of one's faith and seeking to die: between being martyred and being on a suicide mission.

What is at stake here is a hotly contested theological point in contemporary scholarship: how we can understand and appropriate Jesus's sacrifice on Good Friday while also believing that "God is light and in him there is no darkness" (1 John 1:5); that while we hold God permits evil in the world, we reject that God sends it or deals in it. The problem is that some traditional readings of Jesus's death can easily give justification to very few Christians hunting down the martyr's crown because that is what the Father requires.

With all due respect to Sts. Paul, Clement of Alexandria, Anselm of Canterbury, and later John Calvin, many modern

THE LAW OF LOVE

believers cannot baldly accept that the perfect God of love set us up for the fall of Adam and Eve, and then got so angry with us that the grisly death of his only perfect Son was the only way to repair the breach between us.

This is not the only way into the mystery of Holy Week.

Orthodox theologians may be helpful here: They see Jesus's death on Good Friday as the price he paid for the way he lived. Rather than ask, "Why did Jesus die?" they suggest it might be even more confrontational to ask, "Why was Jesus killed?" This puts the last days of Jesus's suffering and death in an entirely new perspective, where Jesus did not simply come only to die. Rather, Jesus came to live, and as a result of the courageous and radical way he lived his life and the saving love he embodied for all humanity, that he so threatened the political, social, and religious authorities of his day that they executed him. But the God of life and love in whom we believe had the last word on Good Friday—Easter Sunday—and raised Christ up that we might all be raised to new life in him and through him.

If suffering and death came to Jesus, then the same will be true for those of us who are persecuted for any reason today for following Christ. We don't go looking for suffering, we are not Christian versions of suicide bombers. Persecution comes to us because of our witness to a faith in Christ that must do justice in the world. By comparison with previous generations, most of us have it easy today, but persecution and martyrdom come to all believers in different ways, in every way we pay the price for holding true to Christ. For us this might mean making serious choices about the company we keep, the business ventures we enter into, the nonviolent protests we mount, the forgoing of luxuries so that others in our world might have necessities, and even remaining faithful to the vows and promises we have made. Suffering might come from the daily routine of looking after a sick child, spouse, or parent; of living with a mental, physical, emotional, or spiritual illness; the scourge of being unemployed, homeless, or addicted; and the feeling that we are unlovable. Christian faith sometimes bites hard, and when it does, we know we are sharing in the martyr's lot. And what should be our response when our faith in Christ costs us something big? "Now my soul is troubled. And what should I say—'Father, save me from this hour'? No, it is for this reason that I have come to this hour. Father, glorify your name" (John 12:27–28). In other words, come what may help me to remain faithful, hopeful, and loving.

BLESSED ARE YOU WHEN PEOPLE REVILE YOU AND PERSECUTE YOU AND UTTER ALL KINDS OF EVIL AGAINST YOU FALSELY ON MY ACCOUNT. REJOICE AND BE GLAD, FOR YOUR REWARD IS GREAT IN HEAVEN, FOR IN THE SAME WAY THEY PERSECUTED THE PROPHETS WHO WERE BEFORE YOU

The ninth Beatitude is clearly related to the eighth because both are concerned with the way in which we may have to suffer for Christ's sake. The word for *revile* that Matthew uses is *oneidízō*, which means "to insult, mock, or cast blame upon another." To make this clearer, Jesus goes on to specify that the type of persecution we may have to endure is regarding what is said, rather than the actions that may be inflicted on us in the previous Beatitude. So, in a nutshell and like the prophets of old, our following of Christ might mean that our reputation gets trashed. It seems particularly odd that Jesus says that if this happens to us then we should "rejoice and be glad." As we have seen, if we understand a blessing to be a gloss over all sorts of tough human realities with, "Well done, keep it up, be happy, and we'll fix it all up in heaven," then the latter part of this Beatitude is like a half-time pep talk to finish the game well. But as we have seen, a *makarios*, a blessing, is the discovery that God is present and active in one's experience, right here and right now, even if we are being abused for the wrong reasons. God is not impervious to our pain and unhappiness, or the great manipulator desiring terrible things to punish us or teach us something, but the one who knows what it is to enter into our human experience and enables us to find meaning and hope in the face of persecution.

This Beatitude reminds us that words matter. If Jesus was speaking to us right now, he might say, *Blessed are you when people unfollow, dislike, or blog against you and share or tweet falsely against you on my account. Rejoice and be glad, for your reward is great in heaven, for if the enemies of the prophets had access to social media, they would have persecuted them in the same way before you.* This is why these laws of love need some updating. But first a story from the sixteenth century about why words matter.

In 1551, the most famous confessor in Rome was St. Philip Neri. Popes and paupers sought his counsel and spiritual direction. One day a famous duchess came to him and confessed the sin of gossip. St. Philip told her to go home and get a feather pillow and return to the steps of the church. He met her there, produced a letter opener, and told the noblewoman to rip open the pillow. As she did, the swirling wind in the square picked up the loose feathers and they danced around the square and down the lanes. St. Philip and the duchess watched in silence as the feathers went everywhere. He then turned to her and said, "Now, go and collect all the feathers." She protested, "They have gone everywhere, I couldn't possibly regather them." St. Philip said,

"So too with your tongue, Madam. You have no idea where your words go, you can never unsay them and never collect them."

We are living the ninth Beatitude in a very different world from any before. One of the greatest tensions in modern society is between the public and the private. It's hard to know where one domain stops and the other starts. Social media has been the disruptor in this space, enabling people to post, share, and tag extraordinary details of their hitherto private lives with billions of people around the globe. Many of these postings are harmless or banal, some have far-reaching outcomes that could never have been foreseen at the time. Some of us have been lulled into a false sense of privacy. It's called *social* media for a reason.

If we are going to be blessed when others say or post all kinds of evil against us falsely on Christ's account, then it might help to remember that the main reason people tear others down is power. To know something about someone and share it with all and sundry puts us in a more powerful position with friends or colleagues. When others feel threatened, they will use every weapon at their disposal to bring us down, in conversation, direct insults, mockery, cynical humor, by suggestion, memes, and posting nasty photographs. The condemnation of others, wherever and however it occurs, is often about projection: as we ignore failings in ourselves, we roundly condemn similar failings in others.

Jesus tells us there is a place for criticism, challenge, confrontation, and correction in the Christian life, but we must lead by example and take responsibility to speak carefully about others in private and public.

CHAPTER 4

THE LORD'S PRAYER

Pray then in this way:

> Our Father in heaven,
> hallowed be your name.
> Your kingdom come.
> Your will be done,
>   on earth as it is in heaven.
> Give us this day our daily bread.
> And forgive us our debts,
>   as we also have forgiven our debtors.
> And do not bring us to the time of trial,
>   but rescue us from the evil one.

(Matt 6:9–13)

The word *political* literally means the "affairs of the city" and it relates to the power relationships that see decisions made in groups. With that as our working definition, then *the* political criterion for Jesus was love. It is often said that prayer is political, and so it is. Therefore, the Lord's Prayer is loaded with examples of how love-in-action leads to an ordering of how power should be exercised. Even though we often reel this prayer off by rote without stopping to think about what we're saying, the Our Father is one of the most challenging and confrontational prayers we could ever utter. We should be careful what we pray for—we might just get it.

Fifty-five elegant words that changed the world and continue to do so. Its brevity and simplicity only add to its dignity. Sometimes we can think that if we want to be serious, we have to say long prayers to be heard by God. In Matthew's Gospel, just two verses before Jesus teaches his famous prayer, he instructs the disciples not to "heap up empty phrases as the Gentiles do" because God already knows what is in our hearts as we start to pray. Less is almost always more, which is a good thing for every parent, preacher, and teacher to remember.

There is one other great example when brevity, elegance, and simplicity changed the world politically, and it has a connection to the Lord's Prayer as well. Do you know how long Abraham Lincoln's Gettysburg Address was? 272 words. It took two and a half minutes to deliver. Do you how long the address before Lincoln's was? The Honorable Edward Everett's "Oration" went for just over two hours. He delivered 13,600 words. With no disrespect to Mr. Everett, no one now remembers a thing he said that day. President Lincoln changed not only the United States of America but the world, expressing the aspirations of every inclusive modern democracy: "that this nation, under God, shall have a new birth of freedom—and that government of the people, by the people, for the people, shall not perish from the earth."

What many people don't know is that the Reverend Thomas H. Stockton, chaplain of the House of Representatives, opened the ceremonies that day at Gettysburg with a prayer. It was long too: 1,021 words, which took eleven minutes to deliver. And what were the final fifty-five words of his longer prayer? The Our Father. Lincoln, who grew up a very devout Baptist, seems to have learned from Jesus that the best way to call for a revolution is to keep it brief.

As important as the Lord's Prayer is, it is not in every Gospel. Mark's Gospel has one verse: "Whenever you stand praying, forgive, if you have anything against anyone; so that your Father in heaven may also forgive you your trespasses" (11:25). St. Paul never refers to it, and John 17 has a long prayer from Jesus in the upper room addressed to the Father, which is often called the High Priestly Prayer, but it shares nothing in common in style or content with the Our Father. In Luke's Gospel the teaching that immediately precedes the giving of the Lord's Prayer is all about how we act, where Jesus tells the now-famous Good Samaritan story in response to the question, "Who is my neighbor?" This is immediately followed by Jesus defending Mary against the traditional roles for women in his day, stating that she had chosen the better part of sitting at Jesus's feet as his disciple. Finally, it is from the fuller version in Matthew's Gospel that we get the Lord's Prayer we use.

Matthew 6:9–13	Luke 11:2–4
Our Father in heaven, hallowed be your name. Your kingdom come.	Father, hallowed be your name. Your kingdom come.
Your will be done, on earth as it is in heaven.	
Give us this day our daily bread.	Give us each day our daily bread.
And forgive us our debts, as we also have forgiven our debtors.	And forgive us our sins, for we ourselves forgive everyone indebted to us.

And do not bring us to the time of trial, but rescue us from the evil one.	And do not bring us to the time of trial.

The above longer version of the prayer does not coincide exactly with what we are used to saying, which is one of the wonderful ironies of the present liturgy: for all our attention to being exact in the English translation we use, when it comes to the Lord's Prayer we still use the 1549 version of the Anglican Archbishop of Canterbury, Thomas Cranmer. Even though this is changing, it remains the only modern context where we use *thees* and the *thys*. It is wonderful poetry, but it's not an exact text:

Our Father,
Who art in heaven,
hallowed be Thy name;
Thy kingdom come;
Thy will be done on earth as it is in heaven.
Give us this day our daily bread;
and forgive us our trespasses as we forgive those who trespass against us;
and lead us not into temptation,
but deliver us from evil.

Whatever version we use, this prayer unites the entire Christian family, and if all 2.1 billion of us lived these fifty-five words, we would, in Christ's name, change the world.

OUR FATHER

Sometimes the smallest details are the most revealing. The Lord's Prayer is addressed to "our" Father, not mine or yours but the collective plural, which means the first loving idea is that we are under one God who encompasses all people everywhere, including family, friends, strangers, and enemies. Consequently, we have a common humanity under this one God, therefore we belong to each other. We go on to declare we belong to God in the most intimate of ways, as members of God's family.

I cannot overemphasize how shocking it must have been to hear the way Jesus talked about God as his Abba. Biblical historians point out that Jesus was the first to apply the everyday word *Abba* for God. *Daddy* in English is not a direct parallel word for *Abba*, but it denotes the sort of relationship Jesus is invoking. Lost on us today, however, is that using that term would have been confrontational in first-century Palestine—far too intimate, far too presumptuous. But it does indicate the sort of relationship Jesus had with the Father, the level of access, communion, affection, and ease. What is even more extraordinary, however, is that Jesus invites his followers to address God in a similar way, and so be invited into the same loving relationship. This begins to reveal the break Jesus made with the images and language for God in prayer used before him. This is our legacy.

Father language for God is not value neutral. Some people cannot say the Lord's Prayer as we have it because of what an earthly father did to them. Tragically, I know victims of clerical sexual abuse in the Catholic Church, where priests are customarily called "Father," who have similar problems. In prayer, the father we address is of course the very best possible, the most perfect father. But people who have known a violent earthly father can understandably find it hard to reclaim this ancient and important image for their prayer.

Given that language is dynamic, however, our consciousness has been raised about the dominance in so much Christian private and public prayer of the masculine pronoun and masculine images. It doesn't worry some people, while for others it can be a great barrier. Rather than neutering God, maybe we should become more comfortable using a variety of images for our public and private prayer. We noted earlier that the Bible's richest veins for images of God is in day-to-day situations—a father, mother, potter, a homemaker, doctor, bridegroom, shepherd, friend, lover, a woman about to give birth, gardener, and healer. Of this group I would be very confident to say that God as mother would cause the most difficulty.

Let me tell you a story where that theory became practice. When I was a newly ordained deacon at Kings Cross, Sydney, in 1993 I had a wonderful pastor, a seventy-one-year-old Irish Jesuit priest called Donal Taylor. Donal never said no to any of my pastoral enthusiasms. He would simply say, "I'd be slow on that one"—which I was to discover was his way of saying "Don't do it!" On the Thursday before Trinity Sunday, while we were praying over the readings for the following weekend, and I was down to preach at all the Masses, he asked, "And what new spin is the young deacon going to put out on the ancient doctrine of the Trinity?" I told Donal that I was going to preach that while Father, Son, and Holy Spirit were privileged names for God in the Christian tradition, they did not exhaust the possibilities, and that God could helpfully be styled as our mother. Doubling over in the chair he said, "I'd be slow on that one."

Kings Cross is the red-light district of Sydney and so the congregations there are a wonderful mixture of all God's children, some of them very colorful indeed. At the Vigil Mass, we had our usual parishioners, 120 young women who were boarders at St. Vincent's Catholic High School, and in the front pew was Con, the most famous homeless person in Kings Cross. During my advocacy for the maternity of God, Con jumped up and expressed what was probably a majority position in the church: "God's not our mother! God's not our mother! Mary's our mother and God's our father." Turning to Fr. Donal, he said, "Father Donal this young bloke hasn't got a clue." And then turned to the congregation and shouted, "And if you are listening to this bullshit, you need your head examined!" and marched out of the church. The congregation erupted with laughter and 120 young women thought this was the best Mass they ever been to, so I looked at Donal, and then the congregation, and said what could only be said in such a situation: "In the Name of the Father and the Son and the Holy Spirit. Amen," and sat down. And as I did Donal turned to his unteachable deacon and mocked me: "I told you to be slow on that one."

Later, over dinner, Fr. Donal asked me, "Are you going to give the same homily tomorrow?" "I am not sure if you noticed," I replied, "but it did not go down treat tonight." "Oh, you leave Con to me. He swore during Mass and I won't have it, so I will warn him off the place for a week. But I want the same homily." "Really?" I replied. "Look, while God our Mother is not my cup of tea, there are those of us who need to hear that just because we name God as Father, it does not mean we have captured God or can control God."

The great medieval mystic St. Julian of Norwich wrote, "For the almighty truth of the Trinity is our Father, for he made us and keeps us in him. And the deep wisdom of the Trinity is our Mother, in whom we are enclosed. And the high goodness of the Trinity is our Lord, and in him we are enclosed and he in us."[1]

When we say Our Father, we are not addressing a guy in the sky. We are saying the most intimate things about God who creates all, embraces all, and loves us all. And that's just where we start in the Lord's Prayer.

WHO ART IN HEAVEN

Until the late nineteenth century, most Christians read the Bible literally. Even though it sometimes contradicts itself, it was the word of God, and so every detail in it had to be factually true. This position has always had problems. For instance, there is not just one creation story—the famous seven-day version in Genesis 1. In Genesis 2, we have another creation story where we are not told how long creation took, but it seems to happen very quickly, and it occurs in a completely different order from Genesis 1. In this second creation account the garden is not perfect but a place of work, wherein some spaces are already dangerous and off-limits. Lesser-known creation stories come later in Psalm 104 and Job 38, where God just places the earth on its axis on the sea. Then in Psalm 74, we are told that God creates the order of the world by first slaying the chaos created by sea monsters.

The Bible's cosmology looks like this:

- The earth was flat, motionless, and sitting serenely at the center of a simple three-layered universe with heaven above and hell below.
- The sun, moon, stars, and other heavenly bodies circled a stationary earth.
- The flat earth rested on pillars.
- The moon emitted light.
- The universe is composed of water.
- Rain occurred when God opened up windows in the sky.

If we are looking for science here, we are in trouble because none of this can be factual. This is the best a prescientific people could do to explain the created order. But this cosmology affects how we understand a phrase like "who art in heaven," because when we say it or think about it, many of us look up to the skies and beyond.

The Old Testament speaks about heaven 246 times (in the New Revised Standard Version) and the New Testament mentions it on 248 occasions. In an incomplete summary, the various authors in the New Testament tell us that heaven

- Is a paradise where Christ is today
- Is a city designed and built by God and suffused with light
- Has twelve pearl gates
- Is made of gold
- Has gems of every kind as its foundations
- Has abundant trees and water of life
- Has in it the mercy seat, a rainbow throne that looks like an emerald, from which comes flashes of lightning and rumblings of thunder, in front of which are the great multitude, clothed in white, from every nation, tribe, and race standing with palm branches in their hands before the throne chanting day and night: Holy, Holy, Holy is the Lord our God.

It's quite a picture.

We are not meant to take any of this literally, nor should we. It is an attempt to describe the indescribable with very limited language. But I have no problem believing in heaven. If we can have one universe, we can have another one. It would be arrogant in the extreme of humanity to assume that the only universe that exists is the one we can presently observe. Though it is highly contested, many secular scientists are now positing that there must be infinite multiverses having different properties and interuniversal laws. These are sometimes described as "parallel," "other," or "alternate" universes. Maybe one of these, for us the preeminent one, is what believers have been grappling to describe for centuries as heaven, where our universe's laws of time, space, motion, and matter count for nothing. It must be logically true that if we can have one universe, we can have another one, and we are not crazy to think that this one, maybe the only other one, is heaven.

I am in good company in believing that heaven is not a place in the sky we go after we die. It is a state of being or a process we enter. Pope Benedict XVI said, "Eternity is not an unending succession of days in the calendar, but something more like the supreme moment of satisfaction, in which totality embraces us and we embrace totality...life in the full sense, a lunging ever anew into the vastness of being in which we are simply overwhelmed with joy" (*Spe Salvi* 12).

So what survives us or goes to heaven when we die?

Nearly all the great world religions believe in a soul, or its equivalent—something that survives the annihilation of the body in death. In an increasingly secular society, it is striking how the word *soul* persists in ordinary conversation. Many nonreligious people use this most religious of terms to describe another person. We often hear how others are lonely, distressed, or lost souls. It can be said that someone has a "beautiful soul" or that a piece of music, a painting, or other works of art "stirred my soul." We describe mellow jazz as "soulful" and still alert others to distress by an SOS, "save our souls." These uses of the word reinforce St. Thomas Aquinas's teaching that the soul makes us human and sets us apart from other animals.

I believe that whatever else might characterize the soul, memory is an integral part of it. Why? There are now theories about how even the memories of the circumstances of our conception and birth have a bearing on the way we live our lives. It is also apparent that even when people seem to have lost their memory or are unconscious, that there is some recognition of some things at a very deep level. Soul as purified memory means that when I meet God in heaven, I will remember who I am and how I lived, and God will remember me. It's also a comfort for us to think that we will be reunited with those we have loved who have died before us, because we remember each other.

I am confident that Our Father in heaven will not deny a homecoming to those of us who faithfully, lovingly, and hopefully live our lives as best as we can. The Scriptures give us confidence to know that God is not concerned with small matters. None of us is ever too far from the compassion and forgiveness of God to take responsibility for what we have done and what we have failed to do, and to undertake a purification of actions and memories. Our soul, or spirit, will enter into a new state of being, the "better country" where every tear is wiped away, where there is no mourning or crying, because in heaven death has passed away.

HALLOWED BE THY NAME

Hallowed is one word that reveals we are using a translation of the Lord's Prayer from Elizabethan England. I wonder if most people connect *hallow* in this prayer with Halloween on October 31, the eve of the day upon which we celebrate the memory of the hallowed, or the holy, saints in heaven. Except in very formal ways like when we refer to a hallowed institution, we don't use the term much anymore. That is, until it was given a younger and modern audience in 2007 when *Harry Potter and the Deathly Hallows* sold 65 million copies. J. K. Rowling tells her readers that the three deathly hallows are the Elder Wand, the Resurrection Stone, and the Cloak of Invisibility. Whoever owns all three hallows gains mastery over death, and so we start to see the intertextuality between her writing and the mystical traditions she has inherited. Rowling uses *hallow* as a noun. The Lord's Prayer uses it as a verb: God's name is to be hallowed, or held in holiness.

The holiness of God's name is a central tenet of the Old Testament. Indeed, it is so holy it cannot be said aloud or written down, because in ancient times to use someone's name was to have power over them. No one has power over God. "Let them praise your great and awesome name. Holy is he!" (Ps 99:3; also Lev 11:44; 19:2; 20:26; and Isa 40:25). "Who is able to stand before the LORD, this holy God?" (1 Sam 6:20). God is not only holy but also other, saving and to be feared. God was not sinful like humanity but holy and pure and so he called his creation out of their wicked ways into the salvation offered to God's chosen people:

> Do not fear, you worm Jacob,
>   you insect Israel!
> I will help you, says the LORD;
>   your Redeemer is the Holy One of Israel.
>   (Isa 41:14)

Finally, God was to be feared:

> The fear of the LORD is pure,
>   enduring forever;
> the ordinances of the LORD are true
>   and righteous altogether. (Ps 19:9)

This is just one of many examples of where we are called to fear the Lord.

Christians may have inherited this Jewish tradition, but it is completely redrawn in Jesus Christ. While the Father, Son, and

THE LAW OF LOVE

Spirit are eternally holy, they have chosen to save us not by being "other" to humanity, but by coming close, being accessible, vulnerable, and available to us for the sake of our salvation. It is impossible to fully grasp Jesus's invitation to love his Abba and to be frightened of God in the way we sometimes are. When I was a child I literally thought "fear of the Lord" meant I had to be petrified of God and be constantly anxious about sinning and breaking the rules. The Hebrew word for fear of the Lord is *yare*, better translated as "reverence" than fear, which puts an altogether different complexion on hallowing God.

A friend of mine once told me that such was the loving respect and admiration he had for his father, the most cutting thing his dad ever said to him was, "I'm disappointed in you. I know you're better than what you've said and done on this occasion." That comes close to helping us translate into our vernacular what fear of the Lord is all about. When we admire and respect someone, we don't want to let them down, we want to emulate their achievements and grow in their esteem. Their love of us doesn't put us down, it builds us up, and it helps us love ourselves. It changes us for the better. This is what our reverence for God is all about. Maybe Rudolph Otto in *The Idea of the Holy* captured this element of our hallowing of God's name best of all when he spoke about the encounter with the numinous. He observed that religious experience leads to the *mysterium tremendum et fascinas*, the mysterious encounter that is both completely overwhelming and urgent, filled with awe, while at the same time irresistibly attractive.[2]

The ascension stories are among the most numinous in the Gospels and therefore the ones that capture how and why hallowedness matters in our lives now. None of the ascension accounts are interested in how or when Jesus got back to heaven. John and Paul never mention it at all. Mark and Matthew have it happening on the same day as the resurrection, and Luke has it occurring forty days after Easter. The one thing on which all the New Testament writers agree is where in heaven Jesus went, and where he is now—at God's right hand. Even to this day, being on someone's right is an honor. Imagine being invited to Buckingham Palace or the White House and finding that you have been placed at the right hand of the queen or the president? In the Old Testament being on the right hand of David, Samuel, or Elijah was to be the anointed and favored one, the true son or daughter. And it survives in popular culture too. *Game of Thrones* may be too explicit for many people, but the central character throughout the long saga, the most important person after the reigning monarch, is called "The Hand of the King." He is regularly just referred to as "The Hand" and wears a coveted pin depicting a hand to designate his authority.

In telling us, then, that Jesus is now at God's right hand, the Gospels use shorthand to state that God affirms everything Jesus was, said, and did on earth, and therefore Christ is the One for us to follow. However, in the Gospels Jesus goes one step further and teaches us that where he is, so shall we be, that he is going to prepare a place for us, and that in and through him we will have life and have it to the full. We hallow God's name and bask in his presence because we celebrate that, just as Jesus was welcomed to God's right hand, so, too, we may be welcomed to the symbolic right hand of Jesus.

And who is already there? The saints in glory. Wonderful then that on the eve of All Hallows' Day, or All Holy Men and Women's Day, we drive away the evil that stops us from following the example of the extraordinary love ordinary people can achieve in Christ. A saint is someone whom the Church believes is in heaven with God. When we say that someone has been canonized, we declare that because of the way they lived their Christian lives God could not deny them heaven, so they have to be on the list (Latin: *canonizare*, the authoritative list) of recognized saints. Wrongly, we often think saints are perfect, but in fact their greatest witness is how they coped with the difficulties of life and how they reflected in a variety of ways the love of God.

We hallow what God has done through them because we may join them. St. Paul thought saints were everywhere. I think he was right, canonized or otherwise. For most of us sanctity and martyrdom will not come in dramatic ways. The daily routine of looking after a sick child, spouse, or parent; of living with a mental, physical, emotional, or spiritual illness; the scourge of being unemployed, homeless, or addicted; and the feeling that we are unlovable brings with it the reality of sharing in the lot of the martyrs and saints. Those in the holy cloud of witnesses saw God in this world and are now fully alive to him in the next.

To hallow God is to want to see that Christ is breaking in on our world at every moment of the day—above us, behind us, before us, within us, beneath us, on our right, on our left, when we lie, when we sit, when we rise, and in every heart, mouth, and ear that reverences the holiness of God (adaptation of St. Patrick's *Breastplate*).

THY KINGDOM COME, THY WILL BE DONE ON EARTH AS IT IS IN HEAVEN

Recently, I saw the digitally reworked film of Queen Elizabeth II's 1953 coronation. This was British ritual at its most brilliant. The sense of flow, dignity, and beauty was quite overwhelming. I was struck by how this rite mirrored the ordination of a bishop. It has a call, oaths, the reception of the Scriptures, the Liturgy of the Word, recitation of the Creed, an anointing, the presentation of the symbols of office leading up to the crowning, the acclamation by the people, an enthroning, the homage of the subjects, holy communion, the *Te Deum*, and then the recessional. It was made explicitly clear that Christ was anointing Elizabeth Alexandra Mary "to govern the Peoples of the United Kingdom of Great Britain and Northern Ireland, Canada, Australia, New Zealand, the Union of South Africa, Pakistan, and Ceylon, and of your Possessions and the other Territories...."

The camera then panned around Westminster Abbey—dukes and duchesses, earls and countesses, anyone who was anyone was there. As I watched, however, I became increasingly uncomfortable. While everything was said to be done in Christ's name, I could only think that Christ would prefer to be anywhere but here. For millennia, in ceremonies like this all around the world, Christ's kingship is often called upon to confirm that God approves of not only this particular monarch or that particular president, but also of the entire social, economic, and religious hierarchy that seems to go with the institution of the state.

Following on from Jesus saying he was a king, "but not of this world," Christians celebrated his reign as that of the Messiah, or the Christ, literally, "the anointed one," the Redeemer King who would defend the rights of the poor and establish an everlasting reign of justice and peace. The notion of Jesus as an earthly king and an anointer of earthly kingdoms came with the conversion of Emperor Constantine in 313. Bishops started to wear the magenta robes of the senators. Churches took on the shape of Roman basilicas, while the government of the Church came to mirror that of the empire. The Christian liturgy imported all sorts of practices popular in the Roman temples and in civic rituals. Within a century, Christian art began to depict Jesus dressed in royal robes, with a crown, a scepter, and an orb. Mary is often presented in similar dress and starts to be called the Queen of

THE LAW OF LOVE

Heaven; by the high medieval period, she is often cloaked in blue, the prerogative of kings at the time.

We cannot change history, but we do not have to be trapped by it either. In the very Scriptures given into Queen Elizabeth's hands we discover Christ our King is not found amid earthly wealth and splendor, but in desperate poverty, in homelessness, in seeking out and saving the lost, in getting down and getting dirty in the service of those who live on the margins of society. I am not convinced that such groups would be welcome or at home in the lavish coronation ceremonies conducted in Christ the King's name in the Westminster Abbeys of our world.

If we take Christ's kingship seriously, we cannot understand it in terms of worldly status. Jesus said, if any of us want to be first, we must be least, and the servant of all. I admire the lifetime of privileged service Queen Elizabeth has rendered and her obvious and sincere Christian faith, but Christ does not anoint any social or ecclesiastical system of privilege and wealth that is extravagant or disordered in its social relationships.

The most moving moment when Jesus speaks of his reign is from the cross, when the good thief simply asks Jesus, "Remember me." Jesus promises that he will. Being remembered by Christ *is* paradise in that he holds every person in this world close; he calls each one of us by name and challenges us to live lives of sacrificial love. It is seen where simplicity is valued, and where there is a right relationship with the earth. It is seen where the poor are recognized as special points of God's revelation to the world.

The test of those who live out the reign of Christ is not whether we are monied or titled, whether we are successful, but that Christ our King calls us to follow him in remembering all people, regardless of who they are, and being prepared to pay the price in fighting for the dignity of each person. And what's our reward for bringing Christ's reign to bear in our world? That Christ will remember us when we come into his kingdom.

We know from the Qumran scrolls, in what they called "the war of the sons of light against the sons of darkness," that around Jesus's time there was great expectation the Messiah would appear and overthrow the Roman oppressors, while others longed for the procession of a great and grand king. These hopes were unrealized in Jesus. No one predicted the way God would send us a Savior—through a thirteen-year-old girl and her nineteen-year-old husband traveling about one hundred miles (160 kms) from Nazareth to Bethlehem in the final weeks of her pregnancy. On arrival, they find themselves homeless, and at least in one tradition, Jesus is born in a cave or a stable where the animals were housed. Imagine the smell. The first witnesses to his birth would be illiterate, non–temple going shepherds, and heaven and earth became one in a poor, defenseless, messy baby who shows us the way out of our own mess, is our truth, and leads us to the fullness of life in this world and the next. By doing so, by God sending "a love letter" in Christ instead of a political agenda, we are offered a transforming, loving, and saving relationship with the Father, Son, and Spirit that has consequences for how we live in this world and the next. In this relationship nothing is wasted in our often-complex lives.

Jesus took the part of the poor, the sick, women, and those who lived on the fringes of society. He challenged the religious authorities of his day and certainly stirred up trouble in many places he went. On the other hand, he rejected violence and taught his followers to pray for their enemies and return good for evil. Jesus showed us that the justice and equality God longs to see in the world comes from a community that is converted by love, not by weapons, fear, or revenge.

When we say we want the reign of God to come on earth as it is in heaven, the implications are enormous for us and for the world. We are challenged to read the "signs of the times" in every generation, stare down powerful forces filled with fear, and be a Church "of the poor for the poor," as Pope Francis has said. It is so easy to allow our faith lives to become compartmentalized. The Lord's Prayer breaks that wide open. For some, religious belief and practice cannot fit into a nice little box that has no discernible influence on the rest of their lives. Coming to church is a privatized affair. What we celebrate each Sunday is supposed to affect all areas of our lives, every day. Though we can try to make ourselves feel better by turning religion into a weekly spiritual bonbon, that is not what Jesus and the martyrs of our faith gave their lives for, and not what we ask every time we say this phrase in the Lord's Prayer.

Sometimes when Christians do not want to link faith and justice, they quote Matthew 22:21: "Give therefore to the emperor the things that are the emperor's, and to God the things that are God's." Rather than undermine our social action, this text supports it, because what is God's encompasses all the emperors of this world, all civil authorities and states. The sense that we can split off our obligations to the gospel from our participation in the affairs of the state is as false as it is dangerous. When our Sunday devotion does not influence our Monday politics, choices, and behaviors, then evil can reign in us and the world.

By all means we should give to Caesar all that Caesar is justly entitled to have for the sake of the common good. A higher allegiance, however, goes to God, who will call all Caesars to account for what they have done and what they failed to do. And might just ask us to explain how the hell we let them get away with it in the first place. Jesus never promised that bringing his reign here on earth was going to be a picnic, just that when we do, we get a glimpse of heaven.

GIVE US THIS DAY OUR DAILY BREAD

Even though I have shared this story before in two of my other books, I want to tell you about the time when giving and receiving bread each day was not a nice theory, but a lived reality.

When I was in Jesuit novitiate in the mid-1980s, the second-year novices were dropped 125 miles (200 kms) from our first house in Australia at Sevenhill in the Clare Valley north of Adelaide, South Australia. The Austrian Jesuits founded it in 1850. It is, to this day, a parish, a retreat house, and, thank God, a very fine winery!

The second years were given enough money for one emergency phone call, and a letter from the novice master for the police explaining who we are and what we're doing. We were, officially, vagrants. With a backpack and a sleeping bag we had to walk the entire way, begging for our food and accommodation each day. In the pursuit of board and lodging we could not tell anyone who we were or what we were doing. We could not trade off being a Jesuit. The novice master told us that if we were invited into someone's home, then, after we have established the extent of their hospitality, we can tell them who we are so that they would not be frightened that they have welcomed Jack the Ripper to stay the night. If the homeowner, however, has offered the garage and a sandwich and then finds out we are Jesuits and so, then, wants to offer the guest suite and a meal at the dining room table, we were told you cannot get an upgrade from economy to first class!

Those ten days were the only time in my life I've known hunger. During winter, would you let me into your house, let me sleep in your garage, or give me some food? I stayed in hostels for homeless men run by the St. Vincent De Paul Society, broke into decrepit schoolhouses, camped out in bandstands, and slept out under the stars.

On day six I arrived in a small country town at 7:00 pm in the teeming rain. I was soaked to the skin. I was drawn by the bright fluorescent cross that hung over what I was soon to discover was the Catholic Church. There was nothing in the rules to say you could not beg from churches. I walked up the presbytery steps and introduced myself to the parish priest. After giving out my spiel, I asked, "Father, I am wondering if you would get me in touch with the local SVDP?" In his wonderful Irish brogue he replied, "You're looking at the local Vincent de Paul." So Father gave me five dollars for dinner and five for breakfast, a towel for a shower, and a bed in the now-unused old school room. Because he never let me into his house, I went on my way the next day without telling him who I was and what I was doing.

On the third last day of the pilgrimage, as it is actually called, I approached the biggest house in the small town of Riverton. There I met Mrs. Mary Byrne, who proceeded to grill me about where I had come from, why I was in such need, and where I was going. I never told a lie, but I was Jesuitical with the truth. After the interrogation she declared, "I think I can trust ya," and ushered me into her home. She told me I could stay in the guest room, have dinner tonight and breakfast in the morning, and then be on my way. I then told Mary who I was and what I was doing. To which she said, "Get outta here!" and for a moment I thought she meant I had to actually get out of there. But Mary quickly went on, "The Jesuits from Sevenhill look after the church here." And then she changed, "You haven't been sent out as a spy, have you?" "No," I said, "Why would you think I've been sent out as a spy?" "Well, you Jesuits are always going on caring for the poor and a faith that does justice in the world, and I though you lot may have been sent out to spy on us to test whether we have been listening to all those social justice sermons all these years." I assured her I hadn't.

I had a great night with all Mary's family, and the next day I was on my way. When I got to the next small hamlet of Watervale in the late Sunday afternoon, I discovered that everyone was off watching or playing in the local football competition. The only person I could see was on the rise of the hill leaving town, where a woman was weeding her front garden beds. I walked up the hill and through her gate and gave out my spiel: "Hello, I'm Richard Leonard and I'm going through to the Clare to get some work on one of the wineries to get my passage back to Sydney. I have nowhere to stay, and nothing to eat, and I'm wondering if you can help me with either or both."

At the end of my speech the woman looked up from her garden and said, "Are you the Jesuit who stayed with Mary Byrne last night? Her daughter is engaged to my son, and I play the organ at Sevenhill Church." And that night the Byrne family came down and joined me and the Briskys for another wonderful dinner in the Riesling Valley of Australia. Being on pilgrimage was looking good.

When I got to Sevenhill I wrote back to that generous pastor telling him that he did not know it, but he had been kind to a Jesuit novice. A short while later a note arrived from the good pastor that read, "The Jesuits taught me at school in Ireland. I hated every single minute of it. If I'd known who you were and what you were up to, I would have kicked your backside and told you to get yourself out of town. Even now the crafty Jesuits have got one over on me. I knew, however, that there was something a little bit different about you, because, let's face it, you were, without question, the most articulate beggar I've ever met in my life."

Though soul-sore by journey's end, on that road I learned more about "give us this day our daily bread" than ever before.

I came to see how intimately related our sharing bread with the actual poor is to our hunger for the Bread of Life. I discovered that in asking God to help me find bread that day, doing penance and fasting, being totally dependent on God's goodness through the undeserved kindness of strangers, helped me feel close to God in a way I had never known before. On receiving bread and somewhere to lay my head, I was overwhelmed with gratitude for the smallest kindnesses that came my way. In stark context, that pilgrimage showed me that the daily bread of the Lord's Prayer is about decluttering our lives of the things that stop us from being broken and shared out for others. "In the Eucharist we receive Christ hungering in the world. He comes to us, not alone, but with the poor, the oppressed, the starving of the earth. Through him they are looking to us for help, for justice, for love expressed in action. Therefore we cannot properly receive the Bread of life unless at the same time we give the bread of life to those in need wherever and whoever they may be."[3]

FORGIVE US OUR TRESPASSES AS WE FORGIVE THOSE WHO TRESPASS AGAINST US

On an eight-day retreat many years ago, a very difficult relationship I was having with another Jesuit came up in my prayer. When I saw my spiritual director, I told him about my feelings and thoughts and poured out the complex and hurtful things that had been said and done. Filled with anger and frustration I asked the older, wiser priest, "What do you think I should do?" "You could try forgiving him," was the perfect reply. Of all the options I had been canvassing, that was not one of them. Eventually I was able to do it, but not easily or immediately. Forgiveness is often a work-in-progress.

This verse has caused some translators sleepless nights. We say "trespasses" in Cranmer's Lord's Prayer, but the original Greek word used in the New Testament is *opheilemata*, which means "a debt that is owed." The word for *trespass*, or sin, is *paraptoma* and it is not used in this verse. Various reputable translations have used words like *sins*, *trespasses*, *debts*, or *wrongs*. It is not just semantics. Generations have grappled with whether Jesus was referring to economic units or to something greater. The consensus now is strongly toward the latter understanding because we could never repay our debt to God for all that has been given to us. Rather than seeing this Beatitude as an impossible call to love, most scholars argue that the image of a debt is helpful in understanding the challenge to forgive. Jesus makes our obligations to forgiveness very clear in the next verse, Matthew 6:14–15: "For if you forgive others their trespasses [*paraptoma*], your heavenly Father will also forgive you; but if you do not forgive others, neither will your Father forgive your trespasses." Maybe Jesus wanted us to have both ideas: that our sin is like a compounding debt—the more we get into it the harder it is to get out of it—as well as trespassing: when we sin, we head into dangerous territory where we should not be.

Whatever the importance of the words, the message is clear. We are asking God to forgive us *as* we forgive others. That prime conjunction used in this sentence, *as*, is extraordinary. This Beatitude is saying that we will discover the extent of God's forgiveness of our sins to the degree we can forgive others their sins. It is incredible that we can sometimes rattle off the whole prayer so casually, especially this verse. Familiarity breeds contempt. As I have said, we should be careful what we pray for, because we might just get it. This is one part of the Lord's Prayer that is easier said than done.

In the previous chapter, when we looked at mercy, I reflected on how central forgiveness is to Christian love. Here I want to reflect on sin in a way that might help us live out this Beatitude more easily. If we are forgiving other's sins, trespasses, wrongs, or debts, then we need to get a good handle on what it is we are called to do.

The Bible gives us two broad concepts for sinfulness: the first is of a transgression, literally "stepping across the boundaries or limits," of going off course or losing our way. The second definition is that of "missing the mark," of not hitting the target for which we were aiming, or that which was rightly expected of us. Using either concept, it is God through the law and prophets who reveals what the limits or the marks are, and how we can account for ourselves. In the Old Testament, God takes transgressions of his law very seriously. At times he rages at humanity's sinfulness and then at other times loves us enough to constantly forgive us and enables us to try again. Eventually, of course, for Christians, the law of love takes human form in Jesus Christ, and by his life we see in action how our own life should be lived.

When we are baptized in Christ, we acknowledge both original sin and original grace. God's love comes alive in us, even though we are aware of how far from that love we stray off course or miss the mark. Though we can do despicable things and make evil decisions, the Christian concept of sin is predicated on our theology of hope, where we focus on the gap between conscience and action in the light of God's forgiveness made real in Jesus. A spiritual director of mine, Fr. Ray O'Leary, used to encourage me to "take your eyes off the sinner and look to the Savior." He was not suggesting that sinfulness didn't matter, but that we can only find a way out of it through Christ. St. John Chrysostom said in his Easter Sermon (c. AD 400): "Let no one mourn that he [*sic*] has fallen again and again; for forgiveness has risen from the grave."

These days when we even mention the word *sin*, some people don't know what it means. Unless we move in churchgoing circles, it is not a word that has much social currency anymore. Alternatively, for people who are churchgoers, they may have heard so many harrowing ideas about sin and their need to repent of it, that when they hear the word they shut down, and won't or can't listen. Some theologians have discovered another word that we can use that perfectly carries the meaning of sin, but enables people to reflect more easily on sin's impact in their lives for the first time, or revisit the idea in a fresh way. The word is *destruction*. When we sin, we can destroy in large or small ways our relationship with God, one another, ourselves, and, as Pope Francis repeatedly teaches, with the created order as well. Sin understood in this way means that we are asking that God forgive us of our destructiveness to the degree we forgive others who act destructively too. This requires great humility, which is not thinking less *of* ourselves, but thinking less *about* ourselves.

In a previous chapter I said that humility was about not wanting to be God, allowing God to be God in our lives, and knowing that we are the creature. When we recognize how our actions can be so destructive on many levels, we should gain the humility to give others a break. Jesus makes this task clear in Matthew 7:1–5:

> Do not judge, so that you may not be judged. For with the judgment you make you will be judged, and the measure you give will be the measure you get. Why do you see the speck in your neighbor's eye, but do not notice the log in your own eye? Or how can you say to your neighbor, "Let me take the speck out of your eye," while the log is in your own eye? You hypocrite,

> first take the log out of your own eye, and then you
> will see clearly to take the speck out of your neighbor's
> eye.

The knowing, free, and intentionally destructive words and actions of others that some of us are called to forgive are major. We cannot minimize what has been said and done, and often it is only through amazing grace that we can confront it and move to healing and peace. In the fifth century, St. Augustine said that forgiveness was like a mother who has two wonderful daughters named Justice and Compassion. In using such a metaphor Augustine knew that forgiveness was not a one-off event, it was a process that involved other virtues as well.

It's easy to be forgiving in the big picture. We can talk strongly about war, peace, and reconciliation. It's quite another to forgive those closest to us. Part of the problem is that we might have accepted the film *Love Story*'s motto, "Love means never having to say you're sorry." The problem for us is that this film's tagline is not Christian. For followers of Jesus the exact opposite is true. We seek opportunities to forgive, and we look to those we have offended to ask for their forgiveness. Jesus doesn't tell us that forgiveness is easy, just necessary, first for us. Sometimes we think when we forgive someone, we are letting them off the hook. It is the other way around: we are letting ourselves off the hook of wanting to settle old scores, take revenge, and exact retribution. There is a true freedom that comes from forgiving someone. Forgiveness is a gift we give ourselves.

It is also good to reject the phrase "forgive and forget." While our memories of atrocious behavior may dim with time or the psychological pain of it may decrease, these days to forget destructive events is considered unhealthy repression, a sign of trauma that needs urgent and gentle care. Dissociative amnesia can be a necessary outcome for psychological protection, but it is never a noble goal. Remembering is one of the most important things God calls Israel to do in the Old Testament, only so they will not make the same mistakes again. The same is true for us. We remember people and events to the degree that we know who and what to avoid in the future, and most definitely make sure that we do not do to others what was done to us. Memories can be protective. What we are trying to achieve is to remember with as much peace as we can. It was once said that we will know when we have forgiven someone when we can recount what was said or done to us without rancor or bitterness. It is not just memories that have such a central role to play in Christian love, but purified memories, which we work on in this life, and are completed through God's love in the next life.

Finally, sin divides but love unites, and so it follows from everything we have just said about purified memories that there is nothing in the Christian concept of forgiveness that demands that we keep associating with those who continue to hurt us. Self-protection and knowing how to limit the damage from dysfunctional relationships and bad behavior are signs of mature Christian faith. It is good to remember that even Jesus knew how to be self-protective. In Matthew's Gospel there are places where his reception is so bad or dangerous that he leaves and never returns. Jesus instructs the apostles to do the same:

> Whatever town or village you enter, find out who in it is worthy, and stay there until you leave. As you enter the house, greet it. If the house is worthy, let your peace come upon it; but if it is not worthy, let your peace return to you. If anyone will not welcome you or listen to your words, shake off the dust from your feet as you leave that house or town. Truly I tell you, it will be more

tolerable for the land of Sodom and Gomorrah on the
Day of Judgment than for that town. (Matt 10:11–15)

So to us. It is perfectly acceptable for those us who are trying to
forgive to decide whether there should be ongoing interaction.
Some relationships are so toxic, some interactions are so destructive, that the most loving and Christian thing we could do for
them and us is to maintain strict boundaries, and more rarely, cut
the ties. Jesus calls us to die unto self, not to kill ourselves. We do
not have to keep lining up to being done over by someone else
in the name of Christian forgiveness. Rather, to ask God to forgive
us as we forgive others means we also make the most life-giving
decisions we can, but we do it in peace and serenity.

AND LEAD US NOT INTO TEMPTATION, BUT DELIVER US FROM EVIL

In December 2017, Pope Francis became embroiled in an
unusual international debate. Following the lead of the French
bishops, the Italian bishops proposed a revised translation for this
verse in the Lord's Prayer, from "lead us not into temptation" to
"do not let us fall into temptation." The pope had to approve
the change, which he did. Happily. When asked about it in an
interview he said, "Lead us not into temptation is not a good
translation….I'm the one who falls. But it's not [God] who pushes
me into temptation to see how I fall. No, a father does not do
this. A father helps us up immediately. It's Satan who leads us into
temptation—that's his department."[4]

A complex debate then raged among biblical scholars,
Greek linguists, and philologists about Matthew 6:13. Most Catholic scholars agreed that it was necessary to read the text against

the wider context of the Gospel and so most concluded that the best translation is "And do not bring us to the time of trial but rescue us from the evil one." Despite this, the English-speaking bishops have decided not to change what we have said for five hundred years.

The observations of the former Archbishop of Canterbury, Rowan Williams, are very helpful:

> We have to see this first of all in the context of Jesus' own day. His teaching often turns back to this idea that a great time of trial is coming....Jesus says to us... don't assume you know how much you're capable of. Pray that when the time of trial comes, when things get really difficult, you will have the resources to meet it. Now the words "lead us not into temptation" don't quite capture all of that because temptation for us tends to mean just a sort of impulse to do unworthy or sinful things. But the word means so much more in its context; it means this huge trial that's coming, this huge crisis that's coming. Lead us not into crisis...until you've given us what we need to face it.[5]

Staying with the prayer as it is in English and even understanding it as the temptation to cut and run when the going gets tough, it's important to remember that temptation is not sin. To be tempted by something is not the same as doing it. Temptations are the allures that make destructive choices look good. In one sense, the bad news is that we know from the lives of the saints that the closer we get to God, the more temptations increase. The good news is that we can learn how to deal with them.

Usually temptations have a context and a history. They can come when we are feeling most deserted and vulnerable, and they normally strike us at the most susceptible points in our character. To deal with them we need to be aware of their pattern, the way they deceive us into believing that the destructive behavior is "not that bad," will be "just this once," or "for one last time." As well, it helps if we are aware of the danger signs in our lives that can weaken our defenses. Tiredness, boredom, anger, alcohol and drug use, lack of good communication, and poor self-esteem are common realities that can leave us more exposed than usual.

We often feel alone when faced with difficult choices and temptations, but especially at these moments, there are four things we need to remember: temptation is not sin. Only when we freely and knowingly choose to act on temptation is sin involved. When we look at our temptations they often appear as good things, but often they have a sting in the tail that is always destructive. We need to be very alert to all the consequences of what we do and say and learn from our experiences. The more we give into temptation, the more immune we become to seeing that there's anything wrong with what we're doing. We can develop whole habits in our living, deceiving ourselves about what we are doing: "it's not that bad." Mystics remind us that we should be wise in how we deal with temptations: name what's going on and attend to the pattern of the temptation quickly and consistently.

Placing our temptations in the wider context of God's grace, we also have a promise from which we can take great comfort: there is no path of temptation along which Jesus has not gone ahead of us to show us we can choose life ahead of death.

The second part of this invocation, deliver us from evil, is connected to the first and is about freedom. Archbishop Williams is helpful again:

> Set us free from all those things, the fears, the sins, the
> selfish habits that keep us prisoner and that make us

unable to face crisis. It probably originally meant save us from the Evil One....And whether or not people these days believe in a personal devil, I think the idea that the principle or the power of evil coming in to make the most of our weakness and our fear, that still makes sense. And we can still quite rightly pray to be delivered from that.[6]

First, and maybe unusually, a humorous story about taking evil seriously: As I mentioned earlier, my first pastoral appointment was to St. Canice's Parish, which included Kings Cross, the red-light district of Sydney. It was the steepest learning curve of my life, but I loved it, except for Halloween, All Souls Day, and any Friday the 13th. Then every nutter in town called in to share his or her experience of evil, the devil, and demonic possession.

On one occasion at Kings Cross, the pastor, Fr. Donal Taylor, SJ, knocked on my door and said in his gentle Irish brogue, "There are two fellas in the parlor who need your particular gifts." And walked away. As I entered the parlor the men said, "Are you the expert? The old priest said he would get the expert for us." I'd been set up.

Bradley and Gary had just moved into Kings Cross. Bradley was a handbag designer and Gary designed women's shoes. They were the campiest men I had ever met. "We've not been able to sleep since we moved into our unit because it's possessed. So we want an expert like you to come and exorcise our home." I would deal with Donal later! I calmly explained that while we sometimes exorcise people, though these days we recommend psychiatry first, we never exorcise places. I did, however, offer to do a house blessing, one of the most ancient and richest rituals we have. We arranged a date for four days hence. "What do we need in preparation?" they asked. I suggested they buy a cross or an icon, have a bowl of water ready to be blessed, and a candle for me to light during the ceremony. When I arrived at their unit, they had bought scores and scores of crosses and icons, now fashioned into a wave along the wall from their front door to the living room. It was spectacular. Then I discovered twenty candles ablaze, and on the table was a vat of water.

After I processed through the house sprinkling the now-holy water about, Bradley told me I'd missed a room. "I don't think so," I said. "The loo, Father," he replied. I wanted to suggest that if I blessed the cistern he would be flushing holy water for days—but I refrained! As I was leaving, they handed me an envelope, which I later found out contained two thousand dollars. When I gave it in to Fr. Donal he didn't miss a beat: "I knew they were quality guys. I hope you invited them to Sunday Mass."

Two weeks later they were back in the parlor. I thought my house blessing had failed, and if they wanted their money back, I had not seen it since. But they had rushed to tell me that their next-door neighbor, Gwen, had arrived home from a three-month overseas cruise that morning, and had come in to welcome them to the building. Gwen told them that their apartment hadn't sold for a year because of the double murder that occurred in their living room. This violent crime had never been disclosed to Gary and Bradley. All they knew was that something was not right in that place. The spirits were unsettled. Since my house blessing, however, they reported that they had slept like babies.

That couple received an out-of-court-settlement of sixty thousand dollars from the real estate agent. When I told Fr. Donal about these developments, he observed, "Well, I think it's only right that the blesser should get 10 percent of the blessings!" Gary and Bradley did better than that. A week later they donated the entire sum to Caritas, the St. Vincent de Paul and St. Canice's Soup Kitchen and became regular parishioners.

I have always liked the accuracy of the baptismal question: "Do you reject evil in all its guises and all its empty promises?" I believe in evil. When I think of the 36,000 people who will die today of malnutrition or the 60 million refugees in the world, or the dark thoughts I sometimes have, I know that evil exists. And it must be logically true that if we can give ourselves to good and love, to God, then we must be able to surrender ourselves to hate and evil, to the devil. I'm suspicious of "the devil made me do it" theology. But the pope says that the devil's handiwork is seen in discouragement, hopelessness, cowardice, negativity, cynicism, and bitterness. The devil is in the details.

When we ask God to deliver us from evil or "rescue us from the evil one," I struggle with the personification of evil. Pope Francis, following St. Ignatius Loyola's lead, talks with ease about the work of the devil, of Satan. My hesitation is strange because I so easily embrace God/good/love coming to us in Jesus Christ. Maybe it's time for me to pray, "I believe; help my unbelief!" (Mark 9:24). Whatever evil's source, whether it is from within me or from without, or a mixture of both, then praying that we be empowered to have courage over discouragement, hope over hopelessness, bravery over cowardice, positivity over negativity, optimism over cynicism, and joy over bitterness is worth praying for every time.

It also reminds us that we need God's protection, which is not a theme emphasized much in Catholic spirituality. Yet especially in John's Gospel Jesus's protection of the flock is a pivotal promise. The possibility of being stolen away from the Christian family is a real one. We know many people who, for a variety of reasons, have left the fold and been seduced into pursuing other leads. Jesus was never under any illusions about what following his lead may cost, how hard it would be when we come to the time of trial and have to confront evil, but he underlines how much we need trust in his protection. We often like to feel so self-sufficient these days that we can bristle when we hear how Christ protects us, but that is precisely what he does through the word, the sacraments, through the Church, and through all of those who love and look out for us. And whether we realize it or not, if we are going to prepare to deal with the trying times in our lives and confront evil head-on, then we need all the protection we can get.

CHAPTER 5

THE GREATEST COMMANDMENT

When the Pharisees heard that he had silenced the Sadducees, they gathered together, and one of them, a lawyer, asked him a question to test him. "Teacher, which commandment in the law is the greatest?" He said to him, "'You shall love the Lord your God with all your heart, and with all your soul, and with all your mind.' This is the greatest and first commandment. And a second is like it: 'You shall love your neighbor as yourself.' On these two commandments hang all the law and the prophets."

(Matt 22:34–40)

LOVE OF GOD

Matthew and Mark (12:28–34) generally agree on the details about this event. Luke certainly records it, but while the substance is substantially the same, it is a lawyer, not a Sadducee, who stands up to test Jesus, and the lawyer responds to Jesus's questions:

THE LAW OF LOVE

Just then a lawyer stood up to test Jesus. "Teacher,"
he said, "what must I do to inherit eternal life?" He
said to him, "What is written in the law? What do you
read there?" He answered, "You shall love the Lord
your God with all your heart, and with all your soul,
and with all your strength, and with all your mind; and
your neighbor as yourself." And he said to him, "You
have given the right answer; do this, and you will live."
(Luke 10:25–28)

Wonderfully for us, Luke is the only Gospel that continues the
interaction between Jesus and his interlocutor by answering
another of the lawyer's questions ("And who is my neighbor?") by
telling the great parable of the Good Samaritan.

Among scholars right now there a dispute about this crucial
teaching regarding the greatest commandment. The problem is
not the content of what Jesus says or confirms—to love God,
neighbor, and self—but idea that this ethical imperative defines
the core business of Christianity at all, and how we go about
fulfilling it in any case. Of the four words used for *love* in the
New Testament (*eros*, romantic love; *storge*, family love; *philia*,
love between friends; and *agape*, sacrificial love), Jesus tells us
to *agape* God, neighbor, and self. It's the highest form of love
there is. A traditional reading of this text can imply that the ability
to *agape* God, self, and neighbor comes from us, that we have
to undertake these tasks because Jesus commands us to do so.
What theologians worry about with this reading is that the initiative to love rests with us, whereas we hold that the impetus to all
love is God working in us and through us.

True love cannot be commanded or conditioned; if it
is not freely given and received, it is not really love....

114

Jesus' "new commandment," given to his disciples just before his death [is] not a demand that they love him, or even the Father, but rather a command (if, indeed, that is the right word for it) to dwell in the love he bears us. Dwelling in that love means allowing it to transform us so that we in our turn love others. In this context, Jesus uses the telling image of a vine and its branches. The nutrient sap of the vine enables the branches to produce fruit, yet the fruit is for the benefit neither of the vine nor of the branches—it is for others. All love originates in God and flows ever outward from there, transforming all who will allow themselves to be suffused by it. It does not turn back in on itself, demanding reciprocation, but pours itself out for the beloved—even for the ungrateful.[1]

It is John, the "beloved" disciple, in whose name, and from whose community, the Fourth Gospel and the Letters are written, who enables us to see that we love God, neighbor, and self only because of the extraordinary giving of God's love in the first place:

So we have known and believe the love that God has for us.

God is love, and those who abide in love abide in God, and God abides in them. Love has been perfected among us in this: that we may have boldness on the day of judgment, because as he is, so are we in this world. There is no fear in love, but perfect love casts out fear; for fear has to do with punishment, and whoever fears has not reached perfection in love. We love because he first loved us. (1 John 4:16–19)

THE LAW OF LOVE

The initiative is entirely with God and so our response to this love is a further extension of the unconditional gift God freely gives. Our response in saying yes to that love, and to keep saying yes to love, means love becomes our way or being, of living, the fundamental option in our lives, not as a divine ethical imperative. "Grace can never be possessed but can only be received afresh again and again."[2]

Even the invitation to love God is more complex in reality than this narrative suggests, because that experience has to be a very different experience than loving my neighbor, which in turn is different than the love that I bear for myself. This is not just semantics. If I am truly allowing God to love me and for love to be my way of being, then what Jesus is saying is that this will be manifest in the love I have for myself and therefore the degree to which I can love others. This has not been the traditional way of reading this invitation, but it is richer. It becomes a question of whether God's love is from within or without.

> We think of grace (God's saving love) arriving like an ambulance, a just-in-time delivery, an invisible divine cavalry cresting a hill of troubles, a bolt of jazz from the glittering horn of the creator, but maybe it lives in us and is activated by illness of the spirit. Maybe we're loaded with grace. Maybe we're stuffed with the stuff. Maybe it's stitched into our DNA.[3]

Let me give you some examples.

First, God's sacrificial love for us. I have always been moved by the theoretical question that could have been asked of Jesus at every stage of his life: "How far will you go, Jesus of Nazareth?" To which he would always reply, "I will go to the end until they know how much we love them." For Christians, the paschal mystery—the life, death, and resurrection of Jesus—is the central paradigm around which our faith in God is constructed. Rather than see each of these as three acts of the drama of our salvation, we have often focused on Jesus's death as the central salvific event. The death of Jesus is a critical moment in God's commitment to us and our human reality, but so are his life and the resurrection. The Word of God did not become one with us as a human being simply and only to die. If that were baldly true, then why did God spare him from the outcome of the most unjust theological story in the New Testament—Matthew's slaughter of the innocents (Matt 2:13–23)? If Jesus had been murdered by Herod at two years of age, then God could have got his blood sacrifice over nice and early. If all God wanted was the perfect blood offering of his only Son for the sake of appeasing his anger, why did Jesus not leave Nazareth, stir up plenty of trouble around Galilee (as he did), and then march straight into Jerusalem and offend everyone and get crucified early on? It would not have been hard. If Jesus had simply been sent "to die," then what was the reason for his hidden years and his years of public ministry? They were not for God's sake, but for ours.

The sacrificial love of God, which sees God emptied out in the humanity of Jesus, affects everything regarding our love of God, neighbor, and self. If Jesus did not simply and only come to die, then we can reclaim the full paschal mystery in this way: that Jesus came to live; and as a result of the courageous and radical way he lived his life, and the saving love he embodied for all humanity, he threatened the political, social, and religious authorities of his day so much that they executed him. Jesus's full and true divinity did not obliterate his humanity, or else he would be playacting at being human. His divinity is seen in and through the uncompromisingly loving, just, and sacrificial way he lived within the bounds of his humanity. We can stand before the cross and listen to Jesus in John's Gospel: "I have come that you may have life, and have it to the full." This life is not about the perfect Son of the perfect Father making the perfect sacrifice to get us back in God's good books, and thereby saving us. Our God does not deal in death, but life.

On Good Friday, we find God-in-Jesus-Christ confronting evil, death, and destruction head-on, and staring it down, so that on Easter Sunday God's light and life would have the last word in Jesus's life, and through him for all of creation. Once we begin to comprehend what God has done for us in Jesus Christ in the power of the Spirit, as best we might try, there is no way we can emulate the sacrificial love of God on our initiative. The bar has been set too high. But God's love invites us ever more deeply to be sacrificially loving in our love of the Trinity, and it remains their love in us, and for us, that enables us to respond in love, not because of a command to obey, but because we are becoming more of what we are destined to be, like God. When this occurs, extraordinary things can happen.

LOVE OF NEIGHBOR

Just as the love that defines the nature of the Trinity bursts out in creation and salvation, so Jesus invites us to follow in the same way so that the love gratuitously given to us by God is offered to our neighbor. The idea of a neighbor in the Old Testament was about members of the chosen people (Gen 12:1–3; 15:1–6). The Jewish law gave instructions for how to deal with Gentiles, travelers, and foreigners (Deut 14:29; 26:12–13; Lev 19:33–34), but the call to be a neighbor was solely toward fellow Jews, culminating in a commandment Jesus would later make his own: "You shall not take vengeance or bear a grudge against any of your people, but you shall love your neighbor as yourself: I am the LORD" (Lev 19:18). This background is important to how Jesus takes this tradition and subverts it.

Earlier in Matthew's Gospel, Jesus indicates the breadth and depth of who our neighbors have to be, and it is definitely not just those in the family:

> You have heard that it was said, "You shall love your neighbor and hate your enemy." But I say to you, Love your enemies and pray for those who persecute you, so that you may be children of your Father in heaven; for he makes his sun rise on the evil and on the good, and sends rain on the righteous and on the unrighteous. For if you love those who love you, what reward do you have? Do not even the tax collectors do the same? And if you greet only your brothers and sisters, what more are you doing than others? Do not even the Gentiles do the same? Be perfect, therefore, as your heavenly Father is perfect. (Matt 5:43–48)

The word we translate as "perfect" is from the Greek word *telos*, which does not mean faultless or flawless in the way we understand perfection. In the Scriptures *téleios* means "to bring something to maturity, to fulfill its aim or purpose."

> It almost sounds blasphemous—suggesting that humans are capable of emulating God's perfection. Yet it is not simply an imitation or emulation. It is more of a participation. God is loving and merciful, and as that loving mercy embraces us, it draws us into its own flow and dynamic. We become merciful and loving,

THE LAW OF LOVE

not because we are imitating God, but because God's
own merciful love is acting in us.[4]

To drive this point home even further, in Luke's Gospel Jesus
goes on to tell the parable of the Good Samaritan. Some of us
remember that in 1980 the then British Prime Minister Margaret
Thatcher claimed that the parable of the Good Samaritan showed
Jesus's endorsement of the benefits of capitalism. "No-one would
remember the good Samaritan if he'd only had good intentions;
he had money as well." Therefore, she surmised the hero of this
famous story is the one who could afford to pay for the victim's
care. She argued that the reason the Samaritan had the where-
withal to do such a charitable act was because he worked hard
and saved his money wisely. Mrs. Thatcher said this central Christian parable was a justification of her government's policies
demanding that unemployed people work for social security and
that they should be educated about saving their pennies. Politicians should be careful of using the Bible to back up their positions. It has a habit of saying the opposite of what they think or
want it to do. Like many people, Mrs. Thatcher reads this parable
in terms of charity, and even then she got it wrong. Jesus says it
is a lesson in mercy, and the one who shows mercy is turning his
sociopolitical world upside down. Revolution is afoot in this story.
This parable is about what we see, whom we love, and what we
want to do about it.

It is not by accident that the phrase "as cold as charity" is
still current. Deciding on who our neighbor is based on our warm
feelings and the glow of our purses may make us feel good, but
it will result in a very wintry experience for the not-so-lucky recipient. When we "do" loving things, we can often remain powerful
and untouched by the situation of those our charity helps. In *The
Screwtape Letters*, C. S. Lewis observes of a friend, "She's the

120

sort of woman who lives for others—you can tell the others by their hunted expression."

The Good Samaritan is not good because he has the money to act as he sees fit. His greatness is that he has eyes to see his enemy as his neighbor, and he is called to sacrificially love him. The Jewish priest and the morality-teaching Levite see the situation but pretend it's not happening and walk on the other side of the road. But the one who really loves is a Samaritan. The use of this group as the role model would have been shocking. It can be lost on us. Samaritans were mixed-race people from the north of Israel who were thought of as inferior and hated by the Jews of the south. So this most unlikely, least-liked person in Israel, a Samaritan, loves as God loves. His love of God is mature enough to fulfill the purpose that God's love for us intends: to go to someone who should be his enemy, touch that person (who would have defiled him) in order to do what he can at the scene of the crime, and then take him or her with him. He sees, judges, and acts, and in doing so breaks nearly every religious and social law in the book.

To love our neighbor is not about the feel-good factor; it is a life-changing encounter, where, sent by the God who has first loved us, we follow his lead in acting mercifully and justly to everyone, bar none. In doing this we are doing no more than following the pattern being shown in God-made-human in Jesus.

In John's Gospel, the account of Jesus' passion, from his last supper, begins thus (John 13:1): "Jesus knew that the hour had come for him to leave this world and go to the Father. Having loved his own who were in the world, he loved them to the end (*eis télos*)." He loved all the way, we might say; completely. And not just to the bitter end as things wound down, but rather to the goal or high point. On the cross Jesus again uses the idea of *télos*: "It is accomplished," he says. *Tetélestai* in Greek: the goal (*télos*) has been reached (John 19:30). He had gone all the way in his mission to express in his living—and now that included dying—the love God has for humanity: a love utterly beyond human calculations; a love that is disarmed, that does not play our power games, that seeks no advantage for itself, that bears everything, even enmity and hatred, without striking back. God revealed, that is to say expressed, that self-emptying love in Jesus, even while human beings were still sinners who preferred alienation from God to the peace with God that was our original state.[5]

Telling Israel that their neighbors included their enemies and that they had to love and pray for them would have been profoundly confrontational. Israel had a formidable list of enemies, including the Egyptians, Amalekites, Edomites, Canaanites, Syrians, Moabites, Ammonites, Midianites, Philistines, Assyrians, Babylonians, Greeks, and the Romans. All of these are described as enemies of the Jews in the Bible. So to us. If we are loved by God, then whoever might be on our list of enemies are seen in a new light. We are invited to reach out to them with love and compassion, discovering the other's dignity and worth.

First-century Palestine was a violent place. The Romans were a brutal occupying force. Israel's neighbors had unjustly invaded the promised land several times. As I explained earlier, toward their enemies Israel lived by the law of retribution from Exodus 21:23–24: "life for life, eye for eye, tooth for tooth, hand for hand, foot for foot," which is also repeated in the Books of Leviticus and Deuteronomy. Revenge was an acceptable way of reestablishing one's honor. No doubt Jesus saw how revenge drives the cycle of violence and wreaks havoc at every level. While inheriting this tradition, he replaces retribution with love.

To love our enemies can be as tough as it gets because it asks us to go against the most seductive part of our human nature: the desire to get even. This entails breaking the cycle of destruction, which has always been endemic in society but has recently found new outlets. For example, there are now several websites dedicated to revenge. Two of the most popular sites carry the names revengeunlimited.com (no longer available) and thepayback.com. The promotion line for one of them said, "Have you been wronged, mistreated, annoyed or ignored? Are you ready for some payback?...Explore our site and find piles of good ideas and novelties. Revenge Unlimited believes that there are people in desperate need of a good dose of humility." And while both sites go on to "recommend good natured pranks and non-aggressive expressions of distaste," it's curious that they link revenge with having a laugh. I only wish we could. We are invited to love the relative we won't speak to, the former spouse against whom we poison our children, the neighbor we delight in annoying, and the work colleague we badmouth because they got the promotion we were after.

Away from the domestic front, it also applies to those who commit criminal acts against us or others, and the enemies of our state. This is why the Church takes a stand against the death penalty and unjust wars. The reality of revenge and retribution on the domestic, national, and international scene is that it solves nothing. It just eats us up, and for the fleeting moment of satisfaction revenge might bring us, it usually continues the conflict, inflames the anger, and distorts us into something much less than God intended. By contrast, Jesus says that his law is to forgive, love, and pray. This principle is neatly summed up in Al-Anon's advice to screaming spouses as they deal with drunken partners: you might not be able to change the other person, but you can change yourself. Stop screaming, reclaim your own dignity, and greet your partner as civilly as possible. What often happens is the change in you leads to a change in those around you.

For us to love our neighbor, especially the ones we do not want to love, it doesn't start with us, but with God's love that enables us to be humble enough to name the cycle of violence within which we participate and, by God's grace, conquer our pride as we reach the goal and aim to which we were created in love.

LOVE OF SELF

As poor as many of us have been in loving God and our neighbor, the last part of Jesus's triple invitation to love may have had the worst outcome of the three. Love of self has had a disastrous history in the Christian story. The central mistake we have made has been to confuse self-love with self-adoration. To adore oneself could not be further from what Jesus is saying, but in our anxiety that our selfishness would take over our love of self, we often promoted the virtues of self-abnegation, self-denial, and penance to the detriment of legitimate and healthy love of self. These latter virtues are good in themselves, but they can easily become destructive and be ends in themselves rather than means to a positive goal. It is only when we possess true love of self that there is a healthy basis for our denials, discipline, and penances. Love of self is not about canonizing a loss of self-control. Jesus shows us by the way he loved his Father, us, and himself that true love always involves sacrifice. If we love our self in the right way, we have the self-control to forgo those things that are most destructive in our lives, and we have the generosity to do for others the things that will enrich their lives. Jesus knew that we can never love and accept others if we reject ourselves.

Jesus links our own self-worth and dignity and the personal love God has for each of us as the context within which we extend that love to others. Just as in the Lord's Prayer, where we ask to be forgiven as we forgive, so here we are invited to love others to the degree that we love ourselves. Everything hinges around the adjective *as*: "love your neighbor *as* yourself," which means that as we rise up to claim our personal dignity in being a daughter or son of God, we do not treat others as our inferiors on the one hand, or allow others to walk all over us on the other.

How did Christianity stray so far regarding the love of self? The New Testament sings the praises of our bodies as God's masterpiece, for example, "For we are what he has made us, created in Christ Jesus for good works, which God prepared beforehand to be our way of life" (Eph 2:10) and "Do you not know that your body is a temple of the Holy Spirit within you, which you have from God, and that you are not your own? For you were bought with a price; therefore glorify God in your body" (1 Cor 6:19–20); but by the end of the apostolic period, the age of martyrs had begun. The community came to celebrate not just those who, like Jesus, had been killed for their faith, but to think highly of those who thought little of their bodies, not just in martyrdom but those who endured torture, suffering, and even those who voluntarily undertook great penances.

Furthermore, even though Paul knows that mandatory celibacy is not required of leaders in the Christian church, he advocates it strongly for some people. In 1 Corinthians 7 he tells the unmarried and the widows to stay that way so they would be free from anxieties. On one level Paul's call to celibacy is utilitarian: the Lord will soon return, so while we wait and work, there is little point to getting married and having a family. In 1 Timothy 3 and

THE LAW OF LOVE

Titus 1:6–9, Paul assumes that the leaders of the church are married men, but tells his closest followers, Titus and Timothy, to be celibate like him for the sake of the mission. But centuries later at the Councils of Elvira (AD 306) and Carthage (AD 309) a law requiring celibacy for holy orders was enacted. Enforcing it was quite another matter. The earliest monks of the fourth and fifth centuries had very ambivalent feelings about the human body. They thought that, generally, it was to be feared as the instrument through which we would sin. They encouraged us to tame it through prayer, mortification, and penance. Their ideas about the body held sway until Thomas Aquinas in the thirteenth century and the Jesuit theologians of the sixteenth century, who argued that while the body can lead us to sin, it can also be a vehicle of God's grace.

In the sixteenth century, Cornelius Jansen denounced Aquinas and the Jesuits and argued that the earlier anti-body and self-denial views were the correct Christian ones. The Jansenist heresy spread like wildfire through Europe, took root in missionary seminaries, and so went around the world. Among many other things, Jansenism placed great emphasis on individual responsibility for sin, the difficulty of obtaining Christ's mercy (whose true humanity was played down), and the belief that our bodies and our desires were evil, and so had to be harshly dealt with to obtain God's favor. Though Jansenism was condemned as heretical by Pope Urban VIII in 1642, it persists in some Christian thinking to this day. However, it is irreconcilable with Jesus's teaching that the love of God, neighbor, and self are the cornerstones of the Christian life. It follows too, that the opposite must be true as well: we cannot call ourselves Christian if we hate God, hate our neighbor or, importantly in this context, hate ourselves.

What does Christian self-love look like today? Some people argue that Western society has already gone too far in the direction of self-love, for example, the obsession with achieving a

sculptured body, the use of steroids, the growth of the diet industry, the adoration of sportsmen and women, and the cult of the
gym and of the sex industry. But they are elements of a culture
addicted to the excesses of egoism and consumed with adoration of self. We are called to love our bodies, not worship them.
Jesus is not calling us to a narcissistic love, where the worship of
the body can be as false a god as Baal.

Moral theologian James Keenan, SJ, argues that a contemporary reclaiming of the virtues in St. Thomas Aquinas helps us
attain the appropriate love of self. Keenan notes that there is a
fourth and surprising virtue that Thomas outlines: justice, fidelity,
prudence, and *self-care*. Regarding self-care Keenan says,

> We each have a unique responsibility to care for our-
> selves, affectively, mentally, physically, and spiritually.
> Some Christian activists may balk at self-care. Some
> could go so far as to note that if Jesus Christ let self-care
> be a cardinal virtue we would never have been redeemed
> by the blood of the cross. But we have every reason to
> believe that the historical Jesus took care of himself; we
> need only think of how often he is contrasted with John
> the Baptizer. Likewise we have no reason to suppose that
> Jesus suffered from lack of self-esteem. In fact, I think we
> can say that it was precisely because Jesus knew the vir-
> tues of fidelity, justice, and self-care that the agony in the
> Garden was so painful. He was a man who loved God,
> humanity, his friends, and himself: his conflict, like all true
> conflicts, was to determine which relationship made the
> greater claim on him."[6]

In the *Summa Theologiae Prima Secundae* questions 35–37,
Thomas talks about four different types of sorrow and how we

can remedy them. Though sorrow may seem an unusual way to explore love of self, I think they provide a helpful guide in making sure that our self-care is the expression of the love of self that Jesus wants us to have. Thomas says that for a joyful life we must work against anxiety, torpor, pity, and envy.

Anxiety. Even though we are living in countries with the highest standards of living, education, and social connection ever known, anxiety, isolation, depression, and suicide are at epidemic proportions. It is a shocking reality that the greatest cause of death in young people under thirty in the developed world is not the abuse of drugs or alcohol or misadventure, but at their own hands. While the reasons for our anxiety and poor mental health are many and complex, Hugh Mackay argues in *The Good Life* that happiness has become an industry that is selling all of us a lie:

> I don't mind people being happy—but the idea that everything we do is part of the pursuit of happiness seems to me a really dangerous idea and has led to a contemporary disease in Western society, which is fear of sadness. We're kind of teaching our kids that happiness is the default position—it's rubbish. Wholeness is what we ought to be striving for and part of that is sadness, disappointment, frustration, failure; all of those things which make us who we are....I'd like just for a year to have a moratorium on the word "happiness" and to replace it with the word "wholeness."[7]

Mackay is not alone. I have lost count of the number of parents who tell me, "I don't care what my kids do, as long as they're happy." Although it may be just a throwaway line, it is a symptom of a deeper anxiety. Why are we setting our children up for such failure? Why don't Christian parents say, "I want my children to be faithful, hopeful, loving, just, and good." Living those virtues will not always lead to happiness—but it will bring something more valuable and precious: joy.

Joy is one of the great themes in the teaching of Pope Francis. Christian joy is not the same as happiness. Christian joy celebrates that we know where we have come from, why we are here, and where we are going. It moves away from trying to find the easy path to confronting the inevitable tough moments in our lives and embracing suffering as an inescapable reality in the human condition. It seeks to be resilient in the face of adversity and it tells us that we are not meant to live isolated lives as "rocks and islands," as the Simon and Garfunkel song has it. There was a good reason why Jesus sent the disciples out in twos. The word Thomas used for anxiety was the Latin word *angustia*, which means "a narrow passage" or "a straightness." Contemporary self-care starts with bending a bit and navigating life together.

Torpor. We may not use the word *torpor* very much anymore, but it literally means "a slowness of movement," where our limbs are heavy, we feel numb. To overcome a torpor of the body, mind, and spirit, we need to be as active as we can. If our bodies are temples of the Holy Spirit given to us to glorify God (1 Cor 6:19–20), then as self-caring Christians we're called to care for our body, not worship it. As believers in a religion of incarnation we take the body seriously. This includes

- Exercising when we can
- Checking what alcohol and other drugs we take
- Going to health professionals and following their advice
- Getting enough sleep
- Being careful of how much negative media we consume

THE LAW OF LOVE

- Taking time for meditation, prayer, and contemplation
- Enjoying beauty with the eye, the ear, and the heart
- Savoring nutritious meals as often as we can

Finally, and most importantly, have at least one goal or an event each week or more to look forward to, aim for, and plan to enjoy. From small moments, to seeing a friend or an occasion that lifts our spirits, having a personal respite draws us onward and upward. These activities need not be self-indulgent, but ward off feeling physically and emotionally drained. Activity of the mind, body, and spirit multiplies itself and builds motivation and confidence: use it or lose it.

Pity. The sort of pity St. Thomas Aquinas warned against was the sorrow that leads to passivity. For instance, if we described the world as a village of one hundred people, it would look like this:

- 61 people would be from Asia, of whom 19 would be from China, 18 from India, 15 people from Africa, 10 from Europe, not quite 9 from South America and the Caribbean, and 5 from North America.
- 33 would be Christians, 22 Muslims, 14 Hindus, 7 Buddhists, and 2 atheists.
- 26 would be under 14, and 8 would be 65 and over.
- 82 would have an average income of U.S. $5,440 a year, with 51 of those living on less than $2 a day, and 18 would have an average income of U.S. $32,470 per annum.
- 75 of the villagers would live in megacities.

- 13 would be malnourished; 22 would be over-weight.
- 40 would lack access to basic sanitation and 13 would lack access to safe drinking water.
- 77 would have mobile phones.
- 33 would have access to the Internet.
- 25 would live in substandard housing or have no home at all.
- 10 would have no job. Of those with jobs, 36 would work in agriculture, 21 in industry, and 43 in the service sector.
- 7 would be unable to read and write.
- 7 will have gone to college or university.
- 3 would be migrants and 4 would be refugees.
- The richest person in our village would own 40 percent of its entire wealth, while 6 people would own half, and 5 of the 6 would come from the United States.[8]

The antidote to pity is empowerment. In the business world *empowerment* is a buzzword. Everyone is supposed to empower someone else. Even salespeople are told to "empower" their customers to buy. This can seem a very modern idea, except as Christians we believe that empowerment has been around as long as our faith. It's one of the hallmarks of loving others as much as we love ourselves. Three factors can stop pity and start empowerment: collective action, imagination, and systematic reflection.

I said earlier that we are not meant to do life on our own, so we need to feel part of groups that are making a positive change in the world. The outreach and development activities of most Christian churches help enormously here. I may not be able to fix the injustices of the world, but rather than wallow in pity, my love

THE LAW OF LOVE

for myself impels me to support those who can on my behalf. We are in this together, and no contribution of any kind is too small to matter.

Imagination is key because there are lots of things in the world I can't explain—scientific things, genetic dispositions, why one human being would love another, how some people can forgive, or how good some of us are to others, asking for nothing in return. I can't explain these things, but I can imagine them because I have witnessed them. Indeed, I can imagine a world where we speak the truth to each other gently and respectfully, where we share from our abundance with those who have nothing, where understanding takes the place of retribution, and where we are empowered by Power itself to be beacons of equality, exemplars of what's best in human nature. With our feet on the ground and turning our eyes to eternity, pity is left behind as solidarity and compassion take its place.

Finally, to move from the passivity of pity to the love of self we need some structured reflection on where the lights and shadows of our own lives might be. One ancient practice is the Examen of St. Ignatius Loyola, where we talk to Jesus as we would to our very best friend. Ignatius encourages us to take time for it around noon and then again at night, but at least at night before we sleep.

There are six simple steps:

1. Be still and become aware of the presence of God.
2. Review the day gently and with gratitude. Walk through the day and note its joys and delights.
3. Pay attention to how we felt in the day: Where were the light and the good moments? Were we alone or with others, in a special setting or an ordinary one? How did it leave us feeling?

4. Look gently at where the dark and the desolate moments occurred. Were we alone or with others, in a special setting or an ordinary one? How did it leave us feeling? Ask for forgiveness if we need to.

5. Choose one feature of the day and ask the Holy Spirit to help us learn from it. Seek God's protection and help, and seek his wisdom in making better choices.

6. Look toward tomorrow and ask God to help us learn what we can from today and make some decisions for tomorrow so that we might have more lightness and less darkness.

This process is not just about looking at the events of the day but patterns that emerge over time. Ignatius believed that there is always a pattern to what gives us life as well as to our destructive behavior. Things never "just happen," so we must capitalize on the good and stare down the pitiful side of our nature. Once we get into this or another process, it enables us to count our blessings and relish them, see the pitfalls in our life and be proactive about changing them, choosing life.

Envy. The final sorrow observed by Aquinas that keeps us from love of self is envy, which he defined as the "sorrow over another's good." Envy is different from jealousy. The latter vice begrudges not having what someone else has. We covet something for ourselves. Envy may start as jealousy, but through anger and resentment sets out to destroy the person who possesses the goods or gifts we desire. One of the seven deadly sins, it deadens the spirit of the envious, kills off relationships, distorts good desires, and can lead to actual death on domestic and international fronts.

The best remedy for envy is gratitude. As we have seen earlier with our village of one hundred people, on every indicator, even if what we are doing is tough just now, most of us live in privileged circumstances. While we might want more of what others have, gratitude keeps us aware of the gifts and privileges we enjoy. As Christians we do not think our blessings are a right, our due, or ours by good fortune. As Christians, we know this is all gift, and we respond to it every day by just being grateful. The people I know who are most grateful are also the most generous when it comes to praising and thanking others. Often the people we find it hardest to praise are the ones to whom we are closest, our wife or husband, children, friends, parents, or members of religious communities. We don't have to be stingy with praise; there will always be enough to go around. We just have to make sure it is sincere.

If we are full of praise and gratitude for the daily things and the people who enrich our lives, then larger moments of recognition and appreciation take care of themselves. A good place to start is to write down all the things for which we are grateful, no matter how small or stupid the list seems. It's our list, and in compiling it we are already praying because our desire to thank God is itself God's gift. Be grateful.

St. Ignatius Loyola also helps in dealing with envy. He saw it as a sign of the bad spirit, the movement within us that leads to sadness, to seeing obstacles as insurmountable, to a lack of self-worth, turmoil, impulsiveness, negativity and agitation, and causes us to regularly give into temptations. If we are prone to envy, Ignatius says we should name it quickly and consistently whenever it happens, learn a new pattern of behavior that will lead to being grateful for what we have, and fight the feeling that we are trapped in this envious and destructive behavior. As we accept God's grace of loving ourselves more, we should notice the signs of the good spirit that is seen in our courage and strength, consolation, inspiration, and peace. We will feel as though obstacles can be overcome and that we are worth something and can contribute good things to the world. Love of self, properly understood, empowers us to change the world for all God's children.

CHAPTER 6

1 CORINTHIANS 13

If I speak in the tongues of mortals and of angels, but do not have love, I am a noisy gong or a clanging cymbal. And if I have prophetic powers, and understand all mysteries and all knowledge, and if I have all faith, so as to remove mountains, but do not have love, I am nothing. If I give away all my possessions, and if I hand over my body so that I may boast, but do not have love, I gain nothing.

Love is patient; love is kind; love is not envious or boastful or arrogant or rude. It does not insist on its own way; it is not irritable or resentful; it does not rejoice in wrongdoing, but rejoices in the truth. It bears all things, believes all things, hopes all things, and endures all things.

Love never ends. But as for prophecies, they will come to an end; as for tongues, they will cease; as for knowledge, it will come to an end. For we know only in part, and we prophesy only in part; but when the complete comes, the partial will come to an end. When I was a child, I spoke like a child, I thought like a child, I reasoned like a child; when I became an adult, I put an end to childish ways. For now we see in a mirror, dimly, but then we will see face to face. Now I know only in part; then I will know fully, even as I have been fully known. And now faith, hope, and love abide, these three; and the greatest of these is love.

(1 Cor 13:1–13)

This text, of course, is among the most widely proclaimed at weddings. Not just because of the power of its theology or the beauty of its poetry, but because it is perfect, but maybe not for the reasons the bride and groom think. St. Paul's "Ode to Love" sells itself. Having introduced the idea of buying and selling in a discussion about marriage, I am sad to say weddings are big business. The average marriage in OECD countries costs U.S. $44,000—that's around $6,500 an hour. The deacon, priest, or bishop is not the one bumping up the price. I have stood between two floral arrangements that cost more than I do. I readily concede I am not as beautiful as the flowers, but I can talk. We now have families who are mortgaging their houses to pay for their children's weddings. While I am delighted that people celebrate this day well with their families and friends, I am anxious that the wedding industry exploits the dream of the best day of our life with a misplaced belief that the amount of money that a family can pay is comparable to the amount of love available, or that the politics of envy that set our expectations for the day outstrip what is just and right.

In fact, I don't know of a Catholic sacrament that has been more influenced by the media's portrayal of it these days, especially on social media, than marriage. It's not unknown for a priest to be taken by surprise when a bride preparing for marriage says that her dress is being modeled on one in a recent movie, or like

THE LAW OF LOVE

Meagan Markel's, and that the reception is going to be "under a marquee, like in *Four Weddings and a Funeral*." The groom sometimes says he wants the music played at the wedding to be what he has heard in a recent episode of a television show. There is, of course, nothing wrong with any of this, but by the end of the conversation it's clear that the media plays more than a consultative role in the decisions being made for the marriage celebrations. It seems like the church is a set, the ritual is the script, and the priest a supporting actor in a matrimonial matinee. I thank God we have this reading from St. Paul to proclaim, because, despite what other people might think about what really matters on the day, what Paul says about love nails what and why we are celebrating at all, and how we should go about it.

Just for fun, before I became a priest, I used to sing at weddings, and sometimes I was asked to sing some very strange things. The seventies and eighties were heady days! In the early eighties many brides asked for Mary Magdalene's big hit out of Jesus Christ Superstar: "I Don't Know How to Love Him."

To which I used to say, if you don't you shouldn't be here. And think of the rest of the chorus:

> And I've had so many men before;
> [*Too much information!*]
> In very many ways;
> [*Oh please, this is getting worse.*]
> He's just one more.

I don't think that's what we want to say at the sacrament of matrimony.

I was also asked to sing "We've Only Just Begun" by the Carpenters, though I think this sacrament is more than "a kiss for luck and we're on our way." Then there were some great requests:

- "That's Amore" (*When the moon hits your eye like a big pizza pie that's amore*), made famous by Dean Martin
- "Love Will Tear Us Apart" by Joy Division
- The show-stopping recessional "Another One Bites the Dust" (*yeah!*)
- "What's Love Got to Do with It?" by Tina Turner
- "I Still Haven't Found What I'm Looking For" from U2
- "You Can't Always Get What You Want" by the Rolling Stones

My all-time favorite was last year, not at a wedding I sang at, but one at which I was presiding. During the signing of the civil registers we heard the Beatles' great hit:

Yesterday
All my troubles seemed so far away
Now it looks as though they're here to stay
Oh, I believe in yesterday.

The love St. Paul is describing in his famous poem is not primarily revealed in what we say or how we feel, but in what we do. Christian love is an intensely practical affair. When we are patient, kind, and gentle with each other, we are obeying the law of love. So too when we forgive each other, tell the truth, and remain faithful, we are responding to the gift of love already given to us by the Trinity.

St. Paul also tells us elsewhere that another fruit of Christian love is self-control. Sacrifice and self-control are really where love comes into its own. The secular world keeps peddling the myth that self-expression is the only way to happiness. Most of us can

THE LAW OF LOVE

see how irrational this position is and how unlivable the world would be if everyone expressed all their feelings and desires as they wished. Sometimes the most loving thing is to do nothing. If we are very angry with friends, for example, abusing them physically or verbally won't help. If we are sexually attracted to our best friend's spouse, having an affair will end in tears. On a more positive note, if we are alert to the poverty in which others live in our world, making sacrifices so that they might have something will not take away from us at all. Self-control is the ally of love and it helps us sort out the appropriate time to undertake the appropriate action, which leads to true joy.

The problem is that self-control doesn't come easily. We need God's grace to train ourselves in its art and practice it regularly and consistently so that we can enjoy seeing the benefits of winning smaller battles before we venture out on larger campaigns. If we cultivate an attitude of self-restraint, we can be sure that when we most need to exercise it, we are in charge of our emotional life rather than it being in charge of us.

If we are going to love sacrificially as St. Paul suggests, then it starts with us deciding whom we actually love and telling them before it's too late. As we have explored earlier, all humanity is invited into the family of God—without exception—knowing that Jesus came, lived, and died that we might find the way out of the cycle of destruction and death in which humanity had become entrapped, that we might be saved. Christ left this world having told the people that he loved that he loved us, and, by belonging to his family and following his example in word and deed, so should we. That is precisely what we celebrate most especially at Christmas, that God was so committed to us he emptied himself and became as we are, so that we might in some measure become what Christ is.

In almost every developed country these days, as church attendance is low and going down, Christmas remains the time when most people want to come to church. I wish they'd come at Easter as well, but they don't. At Christmas we have members of the Catholic secret service who are never seen in church on any other day of the year for risk of blowing their covers.

Tragically it is not unknown for grumpy priests to berate those who actually come to church on Christmas: "We didn't see any of you at Mass last week, and we probably won't see you next week, but you've turned up in droves to sing a carol." If this is meant to shame people into returning to the Church, it only has the opposite effect, reinforcing the feeling that they are being judged and found wanting that stops them coming on any other occasion. It is not the welcoming and inclusive love this great feast day in fact discloses.

In contrast, last year at the Christmas vigil Mass, which thousands of people attended, I went out of my way to welcome everyone home for Christmas. Then I said, "Long gone are the days, thank God, when anyone who is not a regular churchgoer or not a Catholic should feel anything but very welcome in this church. Whether this is the first time you have made it to Mass for a while or whether you belong to another Christian denomination, to another of the world's great faiths, or even if you are an agnostic, secular humanist, or an atheist, and you have come to Mass simply to be with your family, thank you for being so generous. I'd especially like to welcome all the teenagers and young adults. Some of you may be here as unwilling conscripts, just to keep Mum and Dad or Nan and Pop off your back, but I trust you leave as happy as we are that you came."

I was just getting warmed up. "Most of us have no idea what other people brought to this Mass today. Around you there may be victims of clerical sexual abuse. We pray for ever-greater accountability, and for justice and healing. We certainly have families here who have lost a loved one since last Christmas, including children.

THE LAW OF LOVE

There are others here who are living with physical or mental illness, who are desperately lonely, or who are anxious about a sick partner or parent. We are all, in our own way, struggling; so let's lean on each other for support."

Wrapping up, I said, "In fact, I don't care whether you are male or female, rich or poor, black or white, gay or straight, abled or disabled, single or married, or divorced and remarried. God loves us all and the babe of Bethlehem shows us the Way, the Truth and the Life."

After Mass was over, a man stormed into the sacristy. "I'm Jack," he said, "and this is my wife, Mavis, and I didn't like the final part of your welcome." I tried to stay calm. "Jack," I said, "that was over an hour and a half ago and you're still incensed. The sacrament of peace is not having much of an effect. I'm sorry that you don't like women, the poor, black people, the disabled, or the divorced."

"They're OK," he fumed.

"So," I said, "that just leaves straight and gay people, Jack, and I assume because you're married you aren't too bothered about heterosexuals. So that means one word has triggered this eruption."

"Well, you shouldn't have said they're welcome."

"I'm not an idiot, Jack. I chose my words very carefully. I'd like you to point out to me my theological error in saying that God loves us all and that the babe of Bethlehem shows us the Way, the Truth, and the Life."

Mavis piped up, "Jack, I told you not to take on a Jesuit."

That's why Christmas, along with Easter, are moveable feasts of love that are meant to inspire us to a practical service of all. What does this love look like? St. Paul gave us the descriptors.

LOVE IS PATIENT

For all the terrible things colonial powers did, especially to indigenous people and cultures, the English left their colonies many fine cultural legacies. One of the best is the ability to wait in line. English-speaking countries do it better than others. In Paris years ago, I stood in a very long line for a taxi at Gare du Nord train station. I had never seen jostling, shoving, and abuse in my life. And when someone pushed in at the top of the line, all hell broke loose—mainly from an elderly woman holding her poodle! The locals told me this was normal behavior. The success of waiting in line depends on patience, knowing that everything is going as efficiently as possible, and being rewarded at the end for the time and effort expended.

The entire story of salvation hinges on the virtue of patience. The Israelites longed to see the day when the Messiah would come. Each generation hoped and prayed that they would be the one to witness the appearance of God's anointed. Every generation of Jewish people still hope and pray for this. But Jesus did not come as many expected. Some thought he would arrive in a dramatic event and the end of the world would occur. Others expected a regal entrance or a political overthrow of the Romans. Luke's Gospel repeatedly points out that the very people who longed for the day to see the Messiah missed out because they were looking for the wrong signs. John the Baptist is the first to see Jesus for who he really is for the world.

Our love is about the "patient yes," where we stand in line and remind ourselves of how blessed we are to have seen our salvation in Jesus. We remember the faith of those who longed to see what we see and to know what we know. And we cultivate our patience for life's valleys, mountains, and crooked paths, where sometimes we can feel Jesus's absence more than his presence.

Only when we look back can we see he was with us all the way. And as we wait together in line, God's love working in us draws us to say yes to all that salvation holds for us: yes to God's personal love; yes to Jesus's kingdom of justice and peace; yes to every opportunity to serve the gospel, and yes to knowing that our God is a companion to us at every step of our journey, even in the most unexpected ways.

LOVE IS KIND

I won't belabor the point about kindness more here, only because I covered this virtue in chapter 2 on the Ten Commandments in the section entitled, "Be Kind, Be Generous, and Don't Sleep Around." There, I reflected on how important kindness is in the Christian life. I am not the only one who knows how essential kindness is. Some quotes:

- "That's what kindness is. It's not doing something for someone else because they can't, but because you can."—Andrew Iskander
- "What wisdom can you find that is greater than kindness?"—Jean-Jacques Rousseau
- "You can accomplish by kindness what you cannot by force."—Pubilius Syrus
- "Kind words can be short and easy to speak, but their echoes are truly endless."—St. Teresa of Calcutta
- "There is no need for temples; no need for complicated philosophy. Our own brain, our own heart is our temple. The philosophy is kindness."—Dalai Lama[1]

LOVE IS NOT ENVIOUS OR BOASTFUL OR ARROGANT OR RUDE

In the last chapter, we explored the destructive nature of envy, but being boastful, arrogant, and rude are connected to pride, one of the seven deadly sins. St. Paul knew that when we're arrogant or rude, pride is out of control. From personal experience, St. Ignatius Loyola knew that pride is a major block to faith and that we could easily get entrapped by it. Ignatius was once incredibly vain in the pursuit of worldly wealth and status for its own sake. It was a dead end for him, and he suggests it is for all of us. The sin of pride is where we want to be like God—always in charge. Today, we would call proud people, in the sense that Ignatius uses the term, control freaks, trying to control everyone and everything for their benefit or to their will. For Ignatius, the spiritual quest is about staring down the seductive side of our pride and allowing God to refashion it for higher purposes.

Boastfulness creates a similar reality. While here and in 2 Corinthians 11:17, Paul condemns boasting that comes from our overstated sense of self-importance, in 1 Corinthians1 he tells us to boast in the Lord:

> God chose what is foolish in the world to shame the wise; God chose what is weak in the world to shame the strong; God chose what is low and despised in the world, things that are not, to reduce to nothing things that are, so that no one might boast in the presence of God. He is the source of your life in Christ Jesus, who became for us wisdom from God, and righteousness and sanctification and redemption, in order that, as it is written, "Let the one who boasts, boast in the Lord." (vv. 27–31)

THE LAW OF LOVE

So our boast should not be about anything we have been able to achieve but what God has done and is doing in and through us, both individually as well as collectively.

In fact, because these days, given that what most people hear about churches, religions, and faith in the public square is bad news, then boasting in the Lord means that we can communicate the good the people of God do by the power of God's love in the wider community. It is not a question of these canceling out the crimes and shame of what has happened in recent years, rather it is the good spirit who helps us see that the bad news story is not the only story about us, and that as weak and sinful as we are, our witness by action is already there, every day, in season and out of season. Bringing this into the light is not to glorify ourselves, but to highlight that Christ is the teacher, the healer, the Good Shepherd, the one who raises up the poor, and what he achieves through the Church. This is achieved through the network of education, health care, social services, overseas aid development, pastoral retreats, and charitable institutions the Church conducts in Christ's name every day.

LOVE DOES NOT INSIST ON ITS OWN WAY

Paul was big on ambition. Just before this passage on love he writes, "But strive for the greater gifts. And I will show you a still more excellent way" (1 Cor 12:31), and then goes on to teach that for a Christian disciple love is that ultimate way. Like all desires, ambition must be purified. The problem is not in going after a goal, the issue is that our ambition can be selfish, and we end up doing our will rather than the will of God. When we let go and let God work in our lives, we discover that greatness in the world—power, connections, wealth, influence, reputation, and learning—only counts for something in the kingdom of God when it is put at the service of the most vulnerable of our society. That's why the saints and martyrs matter in giving us role models in seeing what amazing grace can achieve. It doesn't mean we do not develop our gifts to the fullest extent possible, but that they are developed for the greater glory of God.

A fine example of developing our gifts for God is found in the 1981 film *Chariots of Fire*, where Eric Liddell, a Scotsman who is a missionary in his evangelical Christian church, is due to compete in the hundred-yard dash at the 1924 Paris Olympics. Because the race is scheduled for Sunday and he cannot run on his Sabbath, a solution must be found to accommodate his informed conscience. One of the best features about this film is the way he sees his body and athletic prowess as a gift from God to be used as a tool for evangelization. "I believe God made me for a purpose, but he also made me fast. And when I run I feel his pleasure....Where does the power come from, to see the race to its end? From within."

To stare down the ego, which often insists on its own way, we must purify our motives. Pedro Arrupe, SJ, thought this involved being attentive to the details of our daily living and making sure that we keep responding in love:

Nothing is more practical than finding God, that is, than falling in love in a quite absolute way. What you are in love with, what seizes your imagination, will affect everything. It will decide what will get you out of bed in the morning, what you do with your evenings, how you spend your weekends, what you read, who you know, what breaks your heart, and what amazes you with joy and gratitude. Fall in love, stay in love, and it will decide everything.[2]

THE LAW OF LOVE

Taming the nagging question, "What's in it for me?" could mean that we receive the promise hundredfold in this world and the next, but it could also mean, "Very little—except living out the love of God," and we strive to do it peacefully either way, because "it's not about me."

LOVE IS NOT IRRITABLE OR RESENTFUL

In previous chapters when talking about forgiveness, I have reflected on how insidious resentment can be. It's like revenge. It eats us up. The odd thing is that we often think that by holding on to resentments we punish the people we resent, when sometimes they don't even sense our resentment. It consumes our energy and good will. Letting go of resentments is not easy. It starts with not taking the speck out of our neighbor's eye while not noticing the log in our own (Matt 7: 3), expressing in a safe way to a trusted person how we feel about the event that has caused the resentment, and then consciously deciding to let go of it. Resentment can take up far too much space in my head. All this is easier said than done.

Irritability is a tough vice to master. Even Jesus got irritated at clueless apostles and disciples (Luke 9:37–56); people's hardness of heart (Mark 3:1–5); Peter's selfish ambition (Mark 8:31–38); the scribes and Pharisees for their abuse of authority (Matt 23:10–12); villages that rejected him (Luke 9:51–55); and hypocrisy (Luke 11:37–54). While this is comforting, we don't have to excuse bad behavior. We must deal with it sooner rather than later because annoyances grow. Irritability comes from a misplaced expectation about how a situation will go or someone might behave. It is about personal power because someone is not doing what I want them to do. We might have every right to be annoyed. If so, then we have to charitably point out the matter and work to resolve it as gently as we can. If we don't do this, then as annoyances compound, we can explode in anger as our irritation increases and we reach our threshold.

It's also good to warn family, friends, and work colleagues about the things that cause us irritation so that they can understand our rising discomfort as these events occur. It helps us keep our emotions under control and in perspective. There is research to suggest that because caffeine and alcohol can lead to pronounced sensitivity, it's best to keep their consumption in check, or at least recognize what happens when we consume them. More positively, because irritability activates our fight-or-flight responses, physical exercise that expels some of our pent-up energy is often helpful. Finally, meditation, silence, and contemplation often enable us to regain a sense of what really matters and help us sort out the person we want to be in the community and the values we want to live. Silence helps us not sweat the small stuff. There is great power in peaceful self-restraint. And even if we never want to hear Elsa sing her hit song from *Frozen* ever again, it's still good to take her advice: "Let it go."

LOVE DOES NOT REJOICE IN WRONGDOING BUT REJOICES IN THE TRUTH

On one level this invitation is obvious. If evil is destructive behavior in all its forms, then a loving person should not participate in it, want or facilitate others' destructiveness, or share knowledge of their words and actions. Material cooperation in sinful actions is real, widespread, and immoral. We can all be enablers for better or for worse. Part of our rejoicing in wrongdoing has a modern echo in the notion of another's bad karma—that they are getting what they deserve. Enjoying someone's comeuppance is a variation on the same theme—that fate has evened up the score for someone else's bad behavior. Enjoying someone else's bad karma or celebrating their comeuppance is rarely charitable. It's a subset of revenge. However, the word *comeuppance* is from the Old English phrase "coming before the judge," and that should temper our rejoicing and explain how we might keep it in check.

The New Testament has a version of karma and comeuppance:

> Do not be deceived; God is not mocked, for you reap whatever you sow. If you sow to your own flesh, you will reap corruption from the flesh; but if you sow to the Spirit, you will reap eternal life from the Spirit. So let us not grow weary in doing what is right, for we will reap at harvest time if we do not give up. So then, whenever we have an opportunity, let us work for the good of all, and especially for those of the family of faith. (Gal 6:7–10)

Rather than hoping that scores will be settled here and now, we believe in faith that all people will be required to account for themselves. We will "come before the judge" and have to own what we have done and what we have failed to do. The only rejoicing for us and for others is that God, our merciful and loving judge, is fully knowing, totally just, and completely compassionate.

The second element in this invitation asks us to rejoice in the truth. In his great hymn *Adoro te devote*, St. Thomas Aquinas writes, "What God's Son has told me, take for truth I do; Truth Himself speaks truly or there's nothing true" (trans. Gerard Manley

Hopkins, SJ). For us to rejoice in the truth we have to want to actively seek it out, warts and all, as best we can. This quest will make for some very challenging times as we question our biases, cultural assumptions, stereotypes, and definitions. We all have them, and they loom large in how we seek and process truth, Christian truth included.

Seeking and seeing the truth is strongly portrayed in the healing of the blind man in Mark 10:46–52. This is especially so in Jesuit dramatist Michael Moynahan's moving story drama entitled *Bartimaeus*. Jesus comes to Jericho and encounters a blind beggar sitting by the roadside. Bartimaeus is a desperate man who acts desperately, continually calling out until he's heard. When Jesus summons him, he asks the blind man one of the strangest questions in the Gospel: "What do you want me to do for you?" Maybe Jesus wants Bartimaeus to name his deepest desire. Maybe Jesus knows that it is, often, the unseen hurt that is the most diseased part of us and needs healing first. Whatever of his motives, Jesus's question gives the man dignity.

In the story drama, the action freezes around this pivotal question: What does Bartimaeus want? As Bartimaeus considers his options, he hears the voices of those he might have to see if he regains his sight. The poor remind him, "If you see me, I could disgust you." The hungry ask, "Do you have the courage to experience and share my hunger?" The elderly inquire whether he wants to see those "put away because we remind you of the frailty of life." The captives challenge him to see those "unjustly bound and oppressed." And finally, the self wants to know, "Are you willing to look inside yourself to see your beauty and ugliness, darkness and light?" It's a gripping scene.

It reminds all of us that sight, and the insight that can come from what we see, bestows on us the dignity of having options and the responsibility to do something about what we behold.

THE LAW OF LOVE

To see and find the truth is a burden, a gift, and a responsibility. Moynahan's story drama finishes, like the Gospel story, with the man born blind asking Jesus for the gift of sight. But in the play, in a powerful twist, as Bartimaeus follows Jesus on the path, he stops, turns, and for the first time sees the human faces behind the challenging voices: the poor, the hungry, the elderly, the captives, the self. Bartimaeus goes back, embraces them all, and together they follow Jesus on the road out of town.

If "what God's Son has told me, take for truth I do," then as we gain the sight and insight to see and embrace Christ's truth, then love also gives us the courage to shoulder such a gift. Because this all sounds very heavy, maybe that's why Jesus tells us to rejoice in the truth. I think all Christians should take joy very seriously. We all know that the Gospels never record Jesus as laughing, but as James Martin, SJ, capably demonstrates in *Between Heaven and Mirth: Why Joy, Humor, and Laughter Are at the Heart of the Spiritual Life*, some of the parables in their cultural context would have been hilarious. This can be lost on us.

Because Christ has found us, and not the other way around, then joy should be our first instinct. If we are happy Christians, we need to tell our faces about it soon. Catholics, especially, can be the gloomiest lot you've ever seen. Our lack of joy can be a symptom of serious spiritual illnesses. It can sometimes show how a believer thinks they must earn God's salvation, or that they must save the world, or that they can never be worthy of God's mercy and love. None of these are laughing matters. They are heresies. Only God saves us through unmerited grace. Though we cooperate in salvation, it is the Trinity who effects the salvation of the world. And there is not a person who is beyond the mercy and love of God.

The sort of joy I am advocating here is not walking around

with a supercilious smile on one's face, pretending we do not have a care in the world. That's a pathology. Christian joy is about knowing where we have come from, why we are here, and where we are going. That should put a spring in our step. Joy is one of the strongest and most distinctive themes in the teaching of Pope Francis. An early sign of the centrality of joy in his thought came eight weeks after he was elected. On May 10, 2013, while preaching at the Vatican, the pope said, "If we keep this joy to ourselves it will make us sick in the end, our hearts will grow old and wrinkled and our faces will no longer transmit that great joy—only nostalgia and melancholy, which is not healthy. Sometimes these melancholy Christian faces have more in common with pickled peppers than the joy of having a beautiful life."

Toward the end of that year, in a homily within the Vatican on October 5, Pope Francis said,

A Christian is a man and a woman of joy. Jesus teaches us this, the Church teaches us this, in a special way in this [liturgical] year. What is this joy? Is it having fun? No, it is not the same. Fun is good, eh? Having fun is good. But joy is more, it is something else. It is something that does not come from short-term economic reasons, from momentary reason; it is something deeper. It is a gift. Fun, if we want to have fun all the time, in the end becomes shallow, superficial, and also leads us to that state where we lack Christian wisdom; it makes us a little bit stupid, naïve, no? Everything is fun…no. Joy is another thing. Joy is a gift from God. It fills us from within. It is like an anointing of the Spirit. And this joy is the certainty that Jesus is with us and with the Father.

Joy comes when we are convinced and convicted not of an ideology but of being on the road following Christ: the Way, the Truth, and the Life, for he himself speaks truly or there's nothing true.

LOVE BEARS ALL THINGS, BELIEVES ALL THINGS, HOPES ALL THINGS, ENDURES ALL THINGS

The critical invitation here is to hope: if we have hope, then we can bear suffering because it is shared, we can believe because it has meaning, and we can endure because we have a future.

For Christians there is a difference between optimism and hope: the optimistic person believes that somehow—either through luck, the actions of others, or one's own efforts—the future will be successful and fulfilling. Christian hope says we work hard with all we have to secure a successful and fulfilling future, and we also trust in God's loving care, knowing that we are connected to a greater narrative (a wider Christian family) and a life yet to come. Christian hope and trust are linked: what Jesus has promised, he will fulfill.

Why does a love that hopes, bears up, believes, and endures matter now more than ever? Because the mental health of society as a whole and especially of our young adults is grim indeed. Something is terribly wrong when, as we have noted earlier, in most developed countries the biggest killer of young adults is now suicide. This is due to many factors but meaninglessness is preeminent among them, defined as the one who feels he or she does not matter in the scheme of things, not to any other person, and not to the community. The increase in meaninglessness is connected to a rise in utilitarianism, individualism, and to personal autonomy. My worth or meaning is gauged by my money and status: "I am what I do," and "No one can tell me what to do, especially with my body." We also know there are several other factors as well: marriage breakdown; the fragmentation of extended families and local communities; "helicopter parents" who leave children feeling anxious and smothered; having so many choices that the young can be immobilized; and being told so strongly, "You can achieve anything you want," that we can have unrealistic expectations and lack of awareness of the preparation and hard work that is needed to achieve our goals.

Social media reveals the contradiction between never having more possibilities for making connections online, and at the same time young adults feeling more isolated than ever. In the online world, "friends" whom one may never have met are considered real friends; "likes," or the lack of them, control self-esteem and mood; and the fallout from addictions, including to online pornography, is devastating. Meaninglessness is born of hopelessness.

In *Christus Vivit* (Christ Is Alive), Pope Francis's postsynodal apostolic exhortation from the 2018 Synod on Young People, the Holy Father links Christian hope to several other factors: encouragement; pursuing dreams; maintaining joy: being forgiven and having compassion; seeking the truth; forming consciences; and being mentored and accompanied here on earth and by the cloud of witnesses in heaven. And he argues against

> those who worship the "goddess of lament."...She is a false goddess: she makes you take the wrong road. When everything seems to be standing still and stagnant, when our personal issues trouble us, and social problems do not meet with the right responses, it

does no good to give up. Jesus is the way: welcome him into your "boat" and put out into the deep! He is the Lord! He changes the way we see life. Faith in Jesus leads to greater hope, to a certainty based not on our qualities and skills, but on the word of God, on the invitation that comes from him. Without making too many human calculations, and without worrying about things that challenge your security, put out into the deep. (*Christus Vivit* 141)

Poignantly, young people, especially at the funerals of their friends who have taken their own lives, respond most to a hope that trusts in God's mercy and love, feeling that they are connected to a greater story, to a welcoming and inclusive Catholic community, and to looking for a life yet to come. Christian hope affirms and celebrates that we know where we have come from, why we are here, where we are going, and that we are not doing this on our own.

In this context how can we witness to Christian hope? We need to keep reminding each other we belong to a worldwide Christian family: 2.42 billion Christians; 1.285 billion Catholics. While not ignoring the despicable acts done by a very few of our community and the cover-up of those crimes, which has bought our family in faith to shame, most of us are doing our best with what we have. That is why we trust in Jesus's promise of life to the full. No matter how tough life gets or when we feel lost—we matter to Jesus and to one another. St. Paul in his letter to the Romans expands on a love that hopes:

Therefore, since we are justified by faith, we have peace with God through our Lord Jesus Christ, through whom we have obtained access to this grace in which we stand; and we boast in our hope of sharing the glory of God. And not only that, but we also boast in our sufferings, knowing that suffering produces endurance, and endurance produces character, and character produces hope, and hope does not disappoint us, because God's love has been poured into our hearts through the Holy Spirit that has been given to us. (Rom 5:1–5)

LOVE NEVER ENDS

A love that can bear up, endure, believe, and hope can only come from holding on to the knowledge that there something greater and bigger than us and that there is a world to come. Because we unashamedly believe in an eternal God of love who invites us to share the next life as well, then we have our feet on the ground as we look to heaven.

I consider that the sufferings of this present time are not worth comparing with the glory about to be revealed to us. For the creation waits with eager longing for the revealing of the children of God; for the creation was subjected to futility, not of its own will but by the will of the one who subjected it, in hope that the creation itself will be set free from its bondage to decay and will obtain the freedom of the glory of the children of God. (Rom 8:18–21)

I said earlier I have no problem in believing in heaven, because if we have one universe, it has to be logically possible to have another one—multiverses: a new form of being, a new state, a changed reality.

THE LAW OF LOVE

I have confident faith that God's love of us is so profound that God could not deny heaven to the many people we know who faithfully, lovingly, and hopefully lived their lives as best as they could. The Scriptures give us confidence to know that God does not concern himself with small matters. But what about the individuals and societies whose behavior destroys other people? What about those who never repent of the sexual abuse of a child, of physical and emotional violence, of being a serial adulterer, or a murderer? What about those who refuse to share from their excess with those who have nothing in our world? And what about those who don't care or don't want to know about the fallout from their apathy or the consequences involved in the luxury of ignorance? None of these people, none of us, is ever too far from the compassion and forgiveness of God, but I am also convinced that God takes our free decisions on serious matters very seriously. Our Catholic theology about heaven, hell, and purgatory enshrines a profound religious truth—that our life here on earth impacts on our eternal life, that it is all connected to something more and greater.

So what happens after our soul leaves our body, "commended to the mercy of God," as we used to say? Does love end then? The great parable of God's mercy is the best place to start. In the story of the prodigal son, we have the worst kid in town making a return and being received by his foolishly loving father. Rather than think of heaven, hell, and purgatory as places where we do time, imagine if they are experiences or states. I wonder if when a goodly number of souls—people who have done their best on earth, according to their lights—make the journey home, the Father rushes out to greet them. They start their speech, but the loving Father cuts them off and welcomes them home. That must be the experience of heaven—welcomed to the eternal banquet!

However, some make the journey home and start the speech, which the loving Father allows them to finish—such has been the enormity of their deliberately chosen, free, and seriously destructive behavior toward others and themselves in this world. At the end of the speech they are forgiven, now fully aware of the gravity of their sinfulness and its impact. It costs us to say, "I'm sorry," and it costs the Father to forgive (like a husband or wife who genuinely forgives the other for adultery). That might be purgatory—an experience in cleansing, of being purged, not in anger or suffering, but in love—painful love as it might be.

And for the very few who have deliberately and knowingly rejected God throughout their lives—God in all his forms: in faith, hope, and love—they make the journey to the Father and come face-to-face with pure love. They do not start the speech, they are not welcomed in, because God respects their freedom so much that he allows them to do what they have done all their lives—see love and walk away. That must be hell—to know pure love and full love, to have glimpsed it, and still turn around and walk away because they always have. The ultimate absence: a remembering soul that saw love and chose otherwise.

A love that endures is founded on how we celebrate that God-in-Jesus-Christ confronted evil, death, and destruction head on, and stared it down, so that God's light and life had the last word in Jesus's life, and through him will also have the last word for us and all of creation. This is why even though we rightly grieve at the funerals of those we love who have died, we only grieve to the degree that we have loved, a belief in a love that endures beyond death.

CONCLUSION

Throughout these pages I have argued that unlike Judaism and Islam, we Christians are not "people of the book" but people of a person. We don't follow a text, as important as the Bible is to us in revelation, but we follow God-in-the-flesh, the Word incarnate, Jesus the Christ. God's definitive act of self-giving to humanity was in body language. Though on hearing it for the first time it sounds overly sentimental, it is nonetheless true that Jesus is God's "love letter" to the world, sent gift-wrapped, express, and priority. We didn't earn nor can ever repay God for this saving communication, this gift that literally keeps on giving for all of eternity. It's our privilege then to respond by grace to God's self-disclosure not primarily by following words about Christ, but by being Christ, embodying ever more the nature of God, which is to love.

St. John said it better than anyone:

> Let us love one another, because love is from God; everyone who loves is born of God and knows God.... God's love was revealed among us in this way: God sent his only Son into the world so that we might live through him. In this is love, not that we loved God but that he loved us...since God loved us so much, we

also ought to love one another. No one has ever seen God; if we love one another, God lives in us, and his love is perfected in us.

By this we know that we abide in him and him in us, because he has given us of his Spirit. And we have seen and do testify that the Father has sent his Son as the Savior of the world....So we have known and believe the love that God has for us. (1 John 4:7, 9–14, 16)

As we noted earlier, Methodist minister Martyn Atkins said that Christians are not meant to be salespeople for the gospel—but we are called to be free samples of it. Now that's a new take on the law of love. Are we up to being loving giveaways of God's body language?

I'm an old teacher, and every old teacher knows that recapping on where we have been consolidates the learning. But I want to do that in a different way. Throughout this book I have purposely told true stories, or made reference to fictional ones, about people who have embodied something of the mystery of God's radical love for the world: me as an awkward seventeen-year-old telling my family that I loved them with mixed results; the ad agency's creative team who tried to "sell" poverty, chastity, and obedience for Christ for life; Tommy the resident atheist in John Powell's class who wondered if he would ever find God, but ended up being found by him instead; Bryan Appleyard breathed new life into ancient wisdom through his "Sinai of the Times"; the Mulberry Bag Company, who had to decide whether we should #winchristmas or ask, "It's Christmas. What are you worshipping?"; Seneca, the second-century philosopher who observed that his rich friends were often the angriest of all, and wondered why; Pope Francis, who has told us that our care of the earth is the

THE LAW OF LOVE

greatest right-to-life issue we are facing; Aunty Mercia, her less-than-marvelous captain, and her truly courageous husband Ken; St. John Paul II in Lima, Peru, who said to the rich and powerful, "I won't simply say share what you have. I will say give it back—it belongs to the poor"; Wladyslaw Szpilman in *The Pianist*, who discovered that beauty can bring forth love and decency even from the hardest of hearts; the survivors of clerical sexual abuse who have reminded us that love and justice must meet, or else we are exposed as noisy gongs and clanging cymbals (1 Cor 13:1); and the family who went to battle at the dining room table about why we should bother saying grace before meals.

Pope Francis reminded us that love and mercy are the flipside of the same coin; Sts. Peter and Paul showed us that it's not where we start that counts, but where we can finish; St. Philip Neri, the duchess, and the pillow revealed that what is in our heart is often on our tongue; Abraham Lincoln's Gettysburg Address showed us that less is so often more; on Trinity Sunday a homeless man who wasn't keen on God-our-Mother helped an older priest ponder God's maternal love; while begging on his way to a winery, a young Jesuit learned about asking for daily bread; Harry Potter opened up a discussion about how *hallow* is more a verb rather than a noun; Fr. Ray O'Leary challenged us to "take your eyes off the sinner and look to the Savior"; and while the evil spirits were driven out of Bradley and Gary's haunted apartment, they made room for the poor.

Hugh Mackay wanted us to be joyful while taking aim at the "happiness industry"; love in action meant seeing the world as it is, and our village of one hundred people is a very unjust place; we sang with "I Don't Know How to Love Him" and "Yesterday, all my troubles seemed so far away"; while *Frozen*'s Elsa told us that sometimes we just have to "Let It Go"; Jack and Mavis didn't have a very happy Christmas until they realized that Christ came for everyone, bar none; Eric Liddell ran for God in *Chariots of Fire*; while the jostling passengers on the taxi line at Gare du Nord demonstrated how patient our love must be; St. Thomas Aquinas taught us "What God's Son has told me, take for truth I do; Truth Himself speaks truly or there's nothing true"; while Michael Moynahan, SJ, dramatized what Bartimaeus might have to see if his eyes are opened; and Pope Francis challenged us that if we are joyful followers of Christ, then we could start by telling our faces about it.

Finally and most importantly, the love revealed completely in Christ is the bedrock of our Christian hope, which is based on this question: How far will you go, Jesus of Nazareth? The answer: I will go to the end until they know how much I love them.

"No, in all these things we are more than conquerors through him who loved us. For I am convinced that neither death, nor life, nor angels, nor rulers, nor things present, nor things to come, nor powers, nor height, nor depth, nor anything else in all creation, will be able to separate us from the love of God in Christ Jesus our Lord" (Rom 8:37–39). And that's why our embodiment of Christ, of us being the loving giveaways of God's body language, enables us, through grace, to look at death in the face and know that it's not goodbye, but, see you later.

LIST OF SCRIPTURE REFERENCES

THE LAW OF LOVE

NOTES

CHAPTER 1: LOVE IS HIS WORD

1. Daniel Madigan, "A Lenten Journey," in *Christian Lives Given to the Study of Islam*, ed. Christian W. Troll, SJ, and C. T. R. Hewer (New York: Fordham University Press, 2012), 259, 265, and 270.

2. Daniel A. Madigan, "The Gospel of John as a Structure for Muslim-Christian Understanding," in *Reading the Bible in Islamic Context: Quranic Conversations*, ed. Daniel Crowther et al. (New York: Routledge, 2018), 253–70.

3. Rowan Williams, "Faith, Force and Authority," ISDglobal, Jan. 31, 2014, https://www.youtube.com/watch?v=WhIjZuFRLeA.

4. John Powell, *The Challenge of Faith* (Allen, TX: Thomas Moore, 1998).

CHAPTER 2: THE TEN COMMANDMENTS

1. Bryan Appleyard, "Sinai of the Times," *The Australian Magazine*, March 7–8, 1998, 22.

2. Appleyard, "Sinai of the Times," 23–25.

3. "Decline of Global Extreme Poverty Continues but Has Slowed: World Bank," September 19, 2018, www.worldbank.org.

4. Jill E. Penley, "God Won't Ask," accessed October 20, 2020, http://www.fnbaldeo.com/HTM-Folders/ask.htm.

CHAPTER 3: THE BEATITUDES

1. Johannes B. Metz, *Poverty of Spirit* (Mahwah, NJ: Paulist Press, 1998), 12.

2. Xenophon, *The Art of Horsemanship*, part 2 (Mineola, NY: Dover Publications, 2013).

3. Rev. John Bell, "Light Looked Down," Christmas response in *Cloth for the Cradle* (Glasgow: Wild Goose, 1998).

CHAPTER 4: THE LORD'S PRAYER

1. Julian of Norwich, the Fourteenth Revelation, in *Julian of Norwich: Showings*, trans. Edmund Colledge and James Walsh (New York: Paulist Press, 1978), 285.

2. Rudolph Otto, *The Idea of the Holy*, 2nd ed. (Oxford: Oxford University Press, 1958).

3. Pedro Arrupe, address to International Eucharistic Congress, Philadelphia, 1976, published in *Justice with Faith Today: Selected Letters and Addresses—II*, ed. Jerome Aixala (St. Louis: The Institute of Jesuit Sources, 1980), 171–81.

4. Quoted in Harriet Sherwood, "Led Not into Temptation: Pope Approves Change to Lord's Prayer," *The Guardian*, June 6, 2019.

5. Rowan Williams, "Reflections on the Lord's Prayer," BBC, August 6, 2009, https://www.bbc.co.uk/religion/religions/christianity/prayer/lordsprayer_1.shtml.

6. Williams, "Reflections."

CHAPTER 5: THE GREATEST COMMANDMENT

1. Daniel A. Madigan, "Our Next Word in Common: Mea Culpa?" in *The Future of Interfaith Dialogue: Muslim-Christian Encounters through a Common Word*, ed. Yazid Said and Lejla Demiri (Cambridge: Cambridge University Press, 2018), 177–91.

2. Rudolf Bultmann, *Essays: Philosophical and Theological*, ed. James C. G. Grieg (New York: Macmillan, 1955), 310.

3. Brian Doyle, "Grace Notes," in *Leaping: Revelations and Epiphanies* (Chicago: Loyola Press, 2003), 52.

4. Madigan "Our Next Word in Common," 185.

5. Madigan, "Our Next Word in Common," 185–86.

6. James Keenan, "Proposing Cardinal Virtues," *Theological Studies* 56 (1995): 727.

7. Hugh Mackay, *The Good Life* (Sydney: Macmillan Australia, 2013), 10.

8. "Global Village," One World Nations Online, accessed October 29, 2020, https://www.nationsonline.org/oneworld/global -village.htm.

CHAPTER 6: 1 CORINTHIANS 13

1. Whitney Hopler, "Famous Quotes on Kindness and Well-Being," George Mason University Center for the Advancement of Well Being, November 1, 2017, www.wellbeing.gmu.edu/articles/11279.

2. *Finding God in All Things: A Marquette Prayer Book* (Milwaukee: Marquette University, 2009).